IT'S NOT ABOUT ME

Discovering that voluntourism is a problem, not a solution

SALLY HETHERINGTON, OAM

© Sally Hetherington 2019

ISBN: 9780648490326

All rights reserved. Except for private study, research, criticism or reviews, as permitted under the Copyright Act, no part of this book may be reproduced, stored in a retrieval system, or transmitted in any form or by any means without prior written permission. Enquiries should be made to the publisher.

Cataloguing-in-Publications entry is available from the National Library of Australia http:/catalogue.nla.gov.au

First edition published 2019 by Elephant House Press.
Second edition published 2021 by Sally Hetherington, OAM.

Original Cover Design by Douglas Lima.

DEDICATION

To the team at Human and Hope Association, thank you for your commitment to developing yourselves and your community. It is because of you that we have been able to achieve so much. I will always be grateful to you for demonstrating that empowerment of local staff is the best way to help in Cambodia.

NOTE

Throughout this book I often don't provide the real names of the people I am talking about, who are marked with an asterisk. This is for one of three reasons.

The first is that the Human and Hope Association will always protect the identity of students under the age of 18 years or those in extremely vulnerable situations.

The second is, throughout this book, I share stories of hardship and challenges, often because of the behaviour and actions of others Out of respect for their identities, I have used pseudonyms where appropriate.

And thirdly, a custom I've come to learn and respect in Cambodia is to address people by other labels, for example, we address people by saying 'Bong' (older), 'Oun' (younger), 'Ming/Y' (Aunty), 'Mia/Bpo' (Uncle), Om/Yay (Grandmother and Grandfather), so I often didn't need to learn people's names, nor did they need to learn mine. And that was fine by me.

CONTENTS

1. From Cambodia, With Love – where it all began 1
2. The First Year 11
3. The Khmer Rouge 27
4. Discovering the Key to Sustainability 44
5. The Unfair Treatment of Women 57
6. Direct Aid and False Promises 66
7. Building up Human and Hope Association 77
8. Crime and Safety 95
9. The Pitfalls of Voluntourism and Poverty Tourism ... 107
10. Creating Our Future 137
11. The Limitations of Life's Circumstances 151
12. A Fork in the Road 162
13. A Distinct Culture 179
14. Time for a Change 193
15. Superstition and Ghouls 204
16. Dengue, road accidents, and illnesses, oh my! 217
17. SO, you want to volunteer 234
18. Celebrate Your Successes 247
19. Stepping Back 265
20. A Cambodian Love Story 286
21. Saying Goodbye 309

Afterword 313
Wait, I'm not finished 316
Acknowledgements 317
References 319

As I drove out of the compound on my red and white motorbike, I burst into tears. Those tears continued on my 30-minute drive home through potholes, flood water and sticky brown mud. As I walked through the battered, wooden door of my second storey house, I sank to the floor and sobbed.

It was over.

I was now redundant.

They didn't need me anymore.

I had dedicated almost four years to the organisation. Four years of blood, sweat, dengue fever, pneumonia, constant gastro and tears.

And it was worth every single hurdle.

Every single setback.

Every single sleepless night.

SALLY HETHERINGTON OAM

1. From Cambodia, With Love – where it all began

WARNING: This chapter contains disturbing information about the Khmer Rouge.

IN 2009, I DECIDED I wanted to go on a holiday. As I was flipping the pages of holiday packages in a brochure I had picked up, a striking image caught my eye. 'Cambodia, the Kingdom of Wonder', the text read, above an image of a centuries-old temple.

That's where I want to go, I decided.

It didn't take any effort at all to convince my relatives to join me on a trip to Cambodia.

A few weeks before our departure, I decided to research into the history of the country that had captured my interest. Sitting down at my computer, I came across something I wasn't expecting.

'Tuol Sleng Genocide Museum – Visit a former Khmer Rouge prison', the website snippet read.

Genocide? In Cambodia, the country I was about to visit? That couldn't be right. I thought I was visiting a country with astonishing temples and luscious green rice fields, not a country that had a history of genocide.

IT'S NOT ABOUT ME

I clicked on the website link and was overcome with emotion seeing photos of shattered skulls, torture weapons covered in dried blood, and barbed wire fences. I was shocked, but I couldn't look away. I spent hours that evening researching the history of Cambodia and was disturbed by what I read.

NOVEMBER CAME AROUND SOON enough, and it was time to head off on our adventure. I hadn't forgotten what I had discovered about Cambodia, but as life went on, I put it to the back of my mind.

We arrived in Siem Reap on a hot and sticky day and checked into a small guesthouse. Located on a semi-quiet main road, it was walking distance to the local markets and not too far from the temples of Angkor. We met up with our tour group and spent the next couple of weeks exploring Siem Reap, Kampong Cham, Sihanoukville and Phnom Penh. We ate spiders (crunchy on the outside, warm and liquidy on the inside), shopped up a storm at local markets, and tanned on the beach.

When we visited Phnom Penh, the capital of Cambodia, we took a tour of the Tuol Sleng genocide museum, the former prison I had come across on Google many weeks ago. As we exited the bus and joined the lines of tourists waiting to get into the compound, I stared in disbelief at the circles of barbed wire that ran along the perimeter of the compound. The beauty of the palm trees was in stark contrast with the unimaginable horror that I knew lurked beyond those walls. As we walked through the building, our tour guide, a survivor of the Khmer Rouge regime that controlled over Cambodia for four years, told us harrowing stories of people who entered the building and were never seen again. There were rusted iron beds, shackles still attached. I imagined innocent Cambodians taking their last breath. We stared in disbelief at blood splattered on the ceilings from head wounds, still evident thirty years later. We listened intently as our tour guide described the torture methods used on up to 20,000 innocent citizens. We browsed rooms full of photos of men, women and children who were held captive in Tuol Sleng and met an untimely death. All but seven captives perished under the ruthless soldiers. Their crime was being educated. Being advocates for freedoms we take for granted. They were government officials, teachers, students, monks, academics, doctors and engineers. As time went on, the soldiers and leaders of the Khmer Rouge regime began turning on each other, and thousands of their own were tortured and executed.

As I walked through the grimy white building, I was overcome with a sense of fear I had never experienced before. I couldn't comprehend how humans could do these unimaginable acts to one another. What did this say about humanity? They had held their captives for months at a time, utilising a torture system that was designed to make their prisoners 'confess' to crimes they most likely hadn't committed. They did this because they believed Cambodia needed to start from 'year zero' and have a clean slate.

The aftermath was devastating. A country left with twenty-five percent less population, traumatised and numb. Still in shock, I began to wonder how this was part of our recent history. It only ended in 1979, seven years shy of when I was born. My thoughts then turned to wondering how a country could possibly overcome a genocide like this. How could they rebuild themselves and overcome the devastation and loss of such a mammoth proportion? As we went to our next destination, Choeung Ek, known widely as 'The Killing Fields', I continued to reflect on the resilience of the country. Here, we witnessed shallow mass graves of captives who had been tortured at Tuol Sleng prison. Bone fragments and teeth protruded from the ground, with remains of clothing draped over the makeshift enclosures. We learnt that babies had been executed by being swung against the 'killing tree'. A large speaker hung from a tree and blasted music to drown out the cries and fears of those who were being executed. On some occasions, there were too many prisoners to execute in one evening, so they would wait in misery for the next night to come and their nightmare to be put to an end.

Witnessing the horrific history of Cambodia, I felt I had to do something to help the country with their recovery. I had learnt that poverty rates were high, tertiary enrolment rates were low, and crime out of desperation was common. Another Australian on our tour told me that she was interested in visiting an orphanage, so assuming this was an effective way to help vulnerable children (spoiler alert: it isn't), we decided to visit one in Siem Reap. Without booking an appointment, we tried our luck by having a tuk-tuk transport us a few kilometres out of town to visit an orphanage that he had suggested. We were welcomed by a Cambodian staff member where he showed us around the orphanage. Walking around, I quickly noticed that the rooms were bare, and our voices echoed among the walls. The staff member told us that the children were all studying either in classes at the orphanage, or at a public school. We came across a twenty-something-year-old Australian volunteer who told us he had been at the orphanage a couple of times over the past two years, and who was training the local social workers. I looked at him with envy, wishing that I could make a positive impact like he was. At the end of the tour, the tour guide sat us down and presented us with a donation form, asking us to make a gift to continue their work. I made a donation, hoping that this small gift could make a difference to local children. After, as we headed back into town, I couldn't stop reflecting on what I had just seen and questioned myself on how I could help Cambodia. I couldn't help but feel that there were countless children in Cambodia who weren't living with much hope for the future. Despite not having a motherly urge in my body, I knew that I had to do something to help these children get an education and have a bright future to look towards. They (nor their parents), couldn't help the card they had been dealt, and that's what made me feel so passionate about helping. With Cambodia slowly healing, it was the perfect opportunity to play my part in their journey forward.

WHEN I RETURNED TO Australia, I was a girl on a mission. I felt compelled to help the children of Cambodia to access education, food and safe shelter, and assumed the best way to do this was through volunteering. I had seen photos on Facebook of other friends who had volunteered overseas, with the smiling faces of children, and decided that was the best way to help. I found a residential home for former street children located in Siem Reap, Cambodia. I completed my application and heard back a few weeks later that I was accepted into the volunteer program, where I would be teaching various subjects to disadvantaged children at the residential home in late 2010, and I was counting down the days until this became a reality.

Having never travelled alone, I was more than terrified of the journey that was awaiting me. How was this middle-class girl going to survive a month with no hot water, no proper medical care, and no McDonalds? Although I was eager to fulfil my dream of helping Cambodians, I couldn't help but fear the unknown. The big day finally came and, with a large backpack, I was dropped off at the airport by my father, ready to embark on my first solo trip.

On the flight, I broke my cardinal rule by accepting candy from strangers but, other than that, things went smoothly. Arriving in Cambodia, I was met at the airport by a tuk-tuk driver who drove me to my hostel. As time went by, I made several friends at the hostel and would spend my free time going on long bicycle rides, visiting the amazing sights Siem Reap had to offer, and drinking and dancing until the early hours of the morning. I realised that life had moved on since the horror of the Khmer Rouge, but the contrast between the bright lights of the clubs and the dilapidated bamboo houses a few hundred metres away still got to me.

I rode my bicycle to the organisation I was volunteering at on the first day. As I walked through the gates, I suddenly felt out of my depth. Watching the children running around the centre, calling out to their friends in a language I had no grasp of, I questioned my ability to stick it out for a month. As the day wore on, however, I felt valued. I knew what I was doing.

During the month, I organised computer classes, helped the students read in the library, and ran workshops on topics such as the environment. Yet, I also spent half my time taking photos and videos of myself doing this good work instead of concentrating on helping the children. I told myself it was to promote the organisation. In hindsight, it was to promote myself. Yes, I admit, I was the Australian girl needing a new Facebook profile picture to show friends and family back home the good I was doing. This was a bucket list item, a rite of passage for us global citizens of the world. I gloated to people I met bar hopping that I was volunteering in Cambodia for a month because, in my eyes, I was contributing to the development of the country. I hung out with volunteers from the countless other organisations in Siem Reap, and we shared stories, glorified our achievements and patted ourselves on the back. Reflecting back on this time, I realised the real reason I was helping was to make myself feel good and look good; not to actually change the children's lives for the better.

The time had arrived, and I was finishing up my last day in this volunteer placement. I bawled my eyes out. What if I hadn't taken the perfect Facebook profile picture? What were those poor children going to do without my average teaching? My time had come and gone incredibly quickly, and I was to be replaced by another volunteer. I made my way to the airport, where I proceeded to cry for most of the journey back to Australia. I suddenly felt empty inside, and I knew I had to return.

ALTHOUGH I HAD ONLY been gone a month, my time in Cambodia changed me. I had a desire to do more and to be more. I wanted to offer my time to those living in poverty and make their lives happier and fulfilled. I wanted to ensure that children in Cambodia were able to access quality education, because that was the key to securing a good job. I knew that if I set my mind to it, I could really make a positive impact on the lives of children in Cambodia.

Almost immediately after returning, I started putting the wheels in motion for a return trip. This time though, I was planning to stay for at least a year. Having met many volunteers during my time in Cambodia, I knew there would be a need in organisations for volunteer coordinators. What better way to help Cambodians than by assisting the foreign volunteers who were there to teach them?

When researching potential organisations to approach, I came across two that caught my eye. One was a school for disadvantaged children, and the other was an orphanage. A few days after contacting the orphanage, I was met with a response saying they would love to welcome me. However, I was expected to pay a fee of several hundred dollars. The school also got back to me, saying they would be glad to welcome me given my experience, as their other volunteer coordinator had recently departed. I told them that I was also in talks with the orphanage when the school explained to me that the orphanage was purely a 'money-making mission'. The children often slept outside with no shelter; they were made to dance for money each evening and were treated as tourist attractions. I reflected on what they said and wondered if there was truth to it. Was the orphanage indifferent to my motivation to make a difference? Did they simply just want money? But why? Wasn't their mission to help Cambodian children be happy, healthy and safe? I didn't know what to do, but thought it was the safest option to arrange a placement with the school. From that day, I began saving the money I would need to fund my trip for an entire 15 months and broke the news to my family and friends that I would be heading overseas for some time.

A few months later, carrying a bulging backpack and mixed emotions, I left Sydney. Little did I know, I wouldn't call Australia home for the next five years, three months, and five days.

2. The First Year

I ARRIVED IN CAMBODIA on a Tuesday, right in the middle of the 2011 floods. When I exited the airport, I spent USD$7 on a taxi after I was unable to find a cheaper tuk-tuk. I was berating myself for spending so much of my limited budget on an air-conditioned taxi when the driver suddenly stopped. *Oh good, we are here,* I thought.

I was wrong.

Although we had arrived in town, we were not yet at the guesthouse I had booked myself into. As I looked out of the window, I realised we were at the edge of the flood water on the road that was parallel to the Siem Reap River. There was no way the taxi would be successful in plunging into the thigh-deep water on the way to my guesthouse.

A flooded Siem Reap in 2011

He told me I would have to get out and find my way to my guesthouse. Carrying 30kg of luggage, also known as all of my worldly possessions, I negotiated with a tuk-tuk driver to take me 500 metres down the road to my guesthouse. After settling on USD$3 for the ride, I climbed into the tuk-tuk and, as I hung on to the armrest for dear life, we started driving.

Two hundred metres down the road, with water splashing up into the tuk-tuk, it broke down. The driver tried numerous times to stand up on his motorbike and kick-start the motor, with the tuk-tuk shaking unstably each time, but wasn't successful. As luck would have it, the driver's friend was travelling along the water-logged road too, and his tuk-tuk was doing just fine. They chatted amongst themselves, then made the decision that I was to switch tuk-tuks. I paid my driver and, with the help of a stranger, successfully made an awkward jump from one tuk-tuk to the other, luggage and all.

The stranger stayed on the tuk-tuk with me, covering my sky-blue backpack while I clenched my jaw and closed my eyes. Lo and behold, we made it to my guesthouse in one piece and relatively dry. The floodwater was dangerously close to overflowing into the lobby, but it never reached that level.

I had finally arrived in the place I was going to call home for the next 15 months.

TRANSITIONING FROM AUSTRALIA TO a low-income country wasn't easy. Arriving in the middle of the 2011 floods, in which approximately 40 people were killed, seemed like a bad omen. Added to that, the week after I had arrived in Siem Reap the electricity went down for five full days. I was battling the bad weather in the daytime and living by candlelight in the humidity in the evenings.

Looking back on this time, the positive was that I loved my job. I was working in an unpaid role as a volunteer coordinator at a school for disadvantaged children. When I came into the role, there hadn't been a volunteer coordinator for many months. I got straight into it, organising the system, familiarising myself with the staff and 100+ students, and talking to volunteers about what *they* wanted. After all, the purpose of my role was to focus on keeping volunteers happy whilst laying down some rules.

A few weeks into the role, a volunteer approached me on her first day.

'Sally, I feel useless,' she said. She continued, 'I don't know why I'm here. I work with a Cambodian teacher who knows what she is doing, so what's the point of me teaching?'

At the time, I didn't see things that way. I saw foreign volunteers as crucial to the success of the organisation. That is the message I had been sold by NGOs, celebrities, and the media, and it is what I truly believed.

As months went by, I settled into the school. I took sick children to the hospital, spending countless hours waiting in line for a doctor to see them and most likely tell us there was nothing to worry about. I replaced volunteers and teachers in classes when no one was available and tried my best to come up with new material for the students that they hadn't been taught before by the countless volunteers who had walked the hallways. I conducted visitor tours, showing foreign tourists around the premises in the hope that they would donate a few dollars, so we would have enough funds to provide the children with breakfast the next day.

I spent my weekends going on bicycle rides around different parts of Siem Reap. It was an honour to explore the centuries-old temples that were in my backyard and to learn about the culture of this beautiful country. I spent the evenings partying, drinking cheap buckets of alcohol with new friends and strangers, dancing on tables and forgetting for brief moments of time that I was living in a country with dirt roads, child beggars, and high poverty rates.

I thought what I was doing was awe-inspiring, and that my work as a volunteer coordinator was central to the development of the school and, really, Cambodia. I couldn't comprehend how the school could survive without my skills and the generous contribution that the foreign volunteers were making.

However, as time went by, I started to realise that wasn't the case.

OUR VOLUNTEER POLICY AT the school was that foreign volunteers had to commit to a minimum of one month to their roles. The reasoning was that it took some time to get settled in and it took a few weeks to make a real impact. I was completely behind this way of thinking because even though I thought volunteers were the saviours for this school and others, I knew that volunteers coming for a few days weren't of benefit to anybody.

There was a student at the school who had attachment issues. Every time a new volunteer would come to her class, she would latch onto them. Then, when the volunteer was about to leave, she would become withdrawn and depressed. She needed consistency in her life, yet by having a different volunteer teacher every month, she wasn't afforded that stability. None of the students were. It was no wonder she ended up married by the time she was 15, yearning for constancy in her life.

A few months into my time at this school, a family came to volunteer. This mother, father, and their two children spent almost two months teaching classes and assisting the Khmer (Cambodian) teachers. What they were doing didn't sit right with me. We were allowing children to come and 'teach' classes, overtaking opportunities for the local staff. I knew that if a child were to come to my work and do my job, I wouldn't feel good about it. By allowing these children, who were both under the age of 10 to volunteer, we were effectively sending the message to the Khmer staff that children could do their jobs, and that their roles were worthless and easily replaceable. In addition to this, the children didn't always follow the rules that our students were expected to abide by, which created double standards.

I brought this up with the director and a foreign staff member who dismissed my concerns and stated that they thought the family volunteer program was a good thing. To this day, I disagree. They were not the only family of volunteers to come through during my time at the school.

Later that year, we had another family come and volunteer and I started to realise that the school was willing to bend over backwards for potential funding. Even though we were working with children who came from marginalised and vulnerable backgrounds, we were allowing volunteers to come in and out of the door for what was becoming shorter and shorter periods of time.

We had a contract with several companies who would send tourists to our school to volunteer with children, often paying exorbitant fees for the opportunity (only some of which would trickle down to the school). Essentially, they were 'voluntourists'. For three months of every year, we only accepted volunteers from a European voluntourism organisation. I would go and collect the volunteers from their hostel, show them around the school, hold an induction workshop, and then they would head off to their classes. As there were six volunteers at a time, some of them had to double up in classes. Some volunteers tried hard to create effective and innovative lessons, whilst others didn't. As they were only in Siem Reap for a short period, many of the volunteers liked to spend their evenings partying. I don't blame them; I also did that when I was volunteering in 2010. The problem was, it appeared that these volunteers had a complete disregard for their work. If you had a staff member constantly coming to work hungover, chances are they would get a warning or be fired. As these people were at the school on a voluntary basis, they didn't always feel that level of responsibility. There were volunteers who didn't show up for work and didn't notify me, those who cut their stints short to go travelling, and others who didn't put any effort into their lessons.

IT'S NOT ABOUT ME

A couple of times each year, social work volunteers would come to the school for three months at a time. Whilst this may seem like a good idea at face value, given Cambodia only had a small number of trained social workers at the time, when delving further, it wasn't. As you can imagine, the culture in Cambodia is very different to Western culture. These Western social work volunteers came over with a particular type of culture that wasn't going to work in the local community. The foreign social workers would drive out to the community with the Cambodian social workers, visiting the homes of people they didn't know or have a trusting relationship with. One day, a Cambodian social worker at the school complained to me that the social work volunteer would sit with her bare feet pointing towards the people they were visiting, which wasn't culturally appropriate. Another time, a female colleague told me how one of the social work volunteers invited herself to a wedding my colleague was attending and, despite not being polite in the culture, my colleague said yes as she didn't want to offend the volunteer. I saw that all too often, even between my colleagues and I; they would go out of their way to please the foreign volunteers, despite going against their own culture and what was best for the beneficiaries. Even though the teachers put on a smile, behind their eyes, I could tell their spirit was changing.

Another thing that didn't sit right with me was that we were using children as tourist attractions. When tourists visited the school, they had to pre-book and sign-in at the gate, which was a policy all NGOs should have. However, we allowed large groups to come and visit the school at the one time, turning the place into a zoo. One day, a group of around a dozen wealthy American tourists came to the school. It was my job to prepare activities that the children and tourists could do together, in the hope that doing so would tug at their heartstrings and open their wallets. For three hours, the children played games and made mosaic art from scrap paper while these tourists took photos and joined in. The children were on show, and essentially 'things' to be played with. I began to realise that what we were doing wasn't right. If this school were in Australia, we would never let strangers come in, once off, for a few hours to play with vulnerable children, and they probably wouldn't expect they could, either. Ethics and standards were being thrown out the window. There was an unspoken belief that Cambodians should count themselves lucky to be in the presence of these 'do-gooders' and should take what they can get.

CAMBODIA IS A PRIMARILY Buddhist country, with over 95% of citizens following Buddhism[i]. However, many NGOs choose to celebrate Christmas. Even though I am Catholic, this frustrates me as this was not part of their belief system. The school I worked for was no exception. For one week over Christmas 2011, a group of high school students from another country came to the school and ran activities for the students. We had to put the other volunteers on the backburner and do everything to please this group of students who had also fundraised for the cause.

This group, all under the age of 18, came over with no chaperones. They didn't dress in line with the Khmer culture and our volunteer standards and acted inappropriately with the students. On their final day, they organised a Christmas Eve party at the school, where the students celebrated a day not recognised in the extensive Cambodian public holiday calendar. The students were fed plenty of food, given presents, and won prizes for games. Cambodians already have their version of Christmas; it's called Khmer New Year and occurs every April. By promoting Christmas, these volunteers were creating an expectation in the students that this celebration was going to happen every year. And it did.

MY JOURNEY IN INTERNATIONAL development started with me participating in voluntourism. I honestly thought I was helping. Looking back, I realise I didn't bring any benefit to the school. What those children from vulnerable backgrounds needed was consistency in their lives. My one month of average teaching didn't give them that. There are some people who go to organisations and do the same thing I did for as little as *one hour*. They visit organisations and 'teach' children topics that they have surely learnt ten times over. Parents are sending their children to study at schools and NGOs in the hope of a better future for them. Often, it can be a struggle to get them to send their children in the first place, as many parents expect their children to look after their siblings, walk their livestock, or look after their roadside stalls. To then provide children with inconsistent and substandard education, just isn't right. Children (and their parents) deserve better.

When I was working at the school, a group of tourists one day turned up without an appointment. I went to the closed gate and looked out at them, already knowing this was going to be an awkward encounter.

'Hello, can I help you?' I asked.

'Yes, hello,' one woman spoke on behalf of the group of four. 'We are from Japan, and we have come to your school to help the children. We have face paint and balloons, so we can paint their faces and play games.'

This was very uncomfortable. I had to try and control my scepticism while I looked at the group, all with cameras around their necks, ready to capture the moment they saved Cambodia with their colourful paints.

'Do you have an appointment?' I asked them, my face wincing, already knowing the answer. Even though the school did permit people to come for short periods of time, I knew that even they wouldn't have allowed this.

'No, we don't,' the woman responded.

'Well, I'm sorry, but we don't allow visitors to come here without an appointment.'

'Oh,' the woman said, then turned to her friends and translated. I watched as their faces dropped, and a look of confusion hit them. It seemed as though they thought that it would be an honour for children to be in their presence, get their faces painted, and have a laugh. They, like many others, were mistaken.

'Can we come in and look around anyway?' she asked me.

'Not without an appointment,' I replied, standing my ground. 'So, if you did want to come for a tour, I will happily show you around, if you organise a day and time with us.'

'Okay, thank you,' the woman responded, that look of confusion still on her face. She and her friends got in the tuk-tuk and drove away while I watched, knowing that they were just going to take their show to one of the other hundreds of schools in Siem Reap.

I began to reflect on the entitlement of these visitors, and how I had previously treated locals in Cambodia. Hadn't I, too, turned up to an orphanage in 2009, thinking that was normal, and I could look around the living quarters of vulnerable children? I was learning a lot on this journey, and I wasn't liking what I saw when I looked in the mirror. I saw a hypocrite.

AS TIME WENT BY, I became more disheartened at the state of the school at which I was working. To source more funds, the minimum volunteer period changed from one month to one week. I was feeling very unhappy and wondering what I was going to do, especially considering my personal values were changing.

Then, one weekend, everything changed. My colleague, Sreylin, invited me to her house for lunch. She lived a couple of kilometres from town with her parents, siblings, in-laws, nieces, and nephews. We ate lunch, then went for a trip to the surrounding villages. After escaping a dog that was chasing our motorbike, our first stop was the local pagoda. As we drove into the compound, I was awestruck by the beauty of the enormous pagoda on my right.

As we walked around this colourful pagoda, we came to a two-storey cream building. Sreylin informed me that it was a nightly English school that her friends had set up the year before. Another organisation had previously held English classes in this building, but due to their rental contract being up, they had departed the building, leaving an absence of English education in the commune. In came a group of friends who decided to do something about this. They spoke a range of beginner to upper-intermediate English, so decided to start nightly English classes, charging the students between USD$0.50 and USD$1 a month to cover their costs of electricity, markers and paper. The organisation was called 'Human Hopes Association', and Sreylin told me that in addition to being run by Khmer volunteers, they also accepted foreign volunteers to come and teach.

As we walked around the building, Sreylin told me that Human Hopes Association needed support to become stronger. They were just scraping by with funding and didn't have the money to register as an NGO with the government, which would cost anywhere up to USD$1,000. I told Sreylin I would think about helping, but first I needed to meet the team to learn more about the organization to make sure I was not repeating the same mistakes. Feeling energised, we continued our tour of her commune, and I began to learn more about the community I would dedicate the next several years of my life helping.

I HAD A MEETING with the director of Human Hopes Association a couple of weeks after Sreylin initially took me there. He was a monk who lived at the pagoda, so he was often on hand to watch over the building. Our initial discussion was that I would help the association by building a website for them. However, over the next month, as I got to know the Khmer volunteers, I realised that *this* was the way that communities in Cambodia were going to develop; by Cambodians running their own organisations. After collaborating with Sreylin and the director, we decided that I would become Operations Manager, and help build up the organisation into a reputable NGO. There were two conditions; we had to stop the foreign volunteer program, and I would eventually make myself redundant.

The combined office and library at Human Hopes Association in 2012.

I had spent the past 14 months working unpaid at the other school and had used most of my savings. However, I knew things would have a way of working out. I sent a resignation email to the director of the other school and parted ways.

MY TIME AT THE school I had moved to Cambodia for wasn't in vain. Without spending over a year working there, I never would have learnt the lessons I did. However, a large part of me still regrets encouraging voluntourism so heavily before I learnt how much harm it was doing. To this day, this school still has volunteers coming in and out the door. I suppose, if I hadn't been there from 2011-2012, it would have been someone else, and they might not have learnt from their mistake and worked so hard to rectify it.

Apart from learning that empowering local staff and having Cambodians lead the way to solving issues in their community, I did learn another big lesson. I learnt I should never risk my integrity for money. Many schools and NGOs in Cambodia don't put the welfare of their beneficiaries first. They are more concerned with getting money into their accounts (a concern we all have), than focusing on whether the ways they go about it are morally the right way. In my time at Human Hopes Association, now Human and Hope Association, I had to make many difficult decisions, but I am proud to say I always put the community members first. That is who we are there to help, after all.

3. The Khmer Rouge

WARNING: This chapter contains disturbing information about the Khmer Rouge.

IF YOU ARE UNDER forty and have never visited Cambodia, chances are you mightn't know much detail about the Khmer Rouge regime. I had never heard about this horrific genocide until I first visited Cambodia in 2009.

Remnants of the mass genocide are still everywhere you look. It is estimated that about 28% of Cambodians experience post-traumatic stress disorder[ii]. Bones from victims of the Khmer Rouge regime are often still discovered, as are mass graves.

Many people don't want to talk about what they experienced during the genocide and afterwards. I don't blame them, as I can't imagine the trauma that they have experienced or the constant fear that it will happen again.

The Khmer Rouge consisted of many people who committed inhumane acts. The leader was Saloth Sar, more commonly known as Pol Pot. Born into a moderately wealthy family, Pol Pot received a good education and gained a scholarship to study radio electronics in Paris. He became attracted to communism during his time in France and joined a communist cell in a secret organisation called the Cercle Marxiste ('Marxist Circle')[iii].

Pol Pot returned to Cambodia in 1953 after failing his exams for three successive years. He spent the next year studying the groups that were rebelling against the Cambodian government, then married and became a teacher at a private college, educating his students in French literature and history.

In 1962, the secretary of the underground communist party was arrested and killed, making way for Pol Pot to become the acting leader and eventually the secretary. Soon after, Pol Pot's name was published by police on a list of leftist suspects, resulting in him fleeing to the Vietnamese border in the south and contacting the Viet Cong camped there who were fighting against South Vietnam.

As time went by, the Khmer Rouge movement grew at a rapid rate, with numerous teachers and students moving to the countryside to join the movement. In 1966, a secret meeting was held renaming Pol Pot's party the Communist Party of Kampuchea. The higher-ranking members decided to establish command zones to prepare for an uprising against the government. Pol Pot transitioned from working as part of a collective leadership to being the absolutist leader of the Khmer Rouge.

Lon Nol, a former Cambodian prime minister, staged a coup in March 1970 to depose Prince

Sihanouk as head of state. The Khmer Rouge, allied with Prince Sihanouk, were aided by the North Vietnamese to defeat Lon Nol's army. The North Vietnamese army withdrew from Cambodia in 1972, with the major responsibilities for the civil war tasked with the Khmer Rouge.

The Khmer Republic government, along with the US, dropped an estimated half a million tonnes of bombs on Cambodia between January and August 1973. As many as 300,000 people died as a result, and this horror caused more people to join the Khmer Rouge in retaliation.[iv]

The Khmer Rouge kept gaining ground and held 85% of Cambodian territory in 1973. The US continued to fight beside Lon Nol's army until 1975, when the capital city of Cambodia, Phnom Penh, fell to the Khmer Rouge. That marked the beginning of almost four years of devastation.

RIK CHORK GREW UP in what she calls a simple family. They weren't rich, nor middle class, nor poor. They had enough food to eat and lived in a house made from thick bamboo.

When she was just 13, Rik's mother died. Like many people in Cambodia, Rik wasn't exactly sure how her mother died, however she says it was due to a problem with her mother's lungs.

After her mother died, life was challenging for Rik. Someone needed to take care of her younger brother and sister and, given she was the eldest child, it needed to be her. At first, Rik took her siblings with her to school, so she could continue studying. However, day after day, the other school children mocked her, saying that she was a young single mother. Rik felt she had no choice but to stop studying in grade six.

Rik spent her days looking after her siblings and occasionally helping her father take care of their farm. She longed to have her own market stall, but her father forbade it. His reasoning was that they had enough food to eat, so there was no need for her to work.

As time went by, Cambodia became more unstable. When she was still at school, Rik's teacher used to tell her class that there would be a war; that Lon Nol was planning to force the King out and hold control of the country. Her teacher presented them with chilling words: 'If war happens, be calm, quiet, and patient. Concentrate on surviving and use your willpower not to kill yourselves. Just try your best to live.'

Every few days, Rik would hear of bombings and gun fights around Siem Reap. She recalls bombs that looked like flowers being shot from far away that would land in her village. Her family dug a trench deep in their land to hide in and would take their food in there and wait for the bombing to finish. Although they remained safe, many people in Rik's village died. One time after retreating from their trench, they saw that their neighbour had been decapitated by a bomb whilst eating his rice. Rik lived her life feeling scared and worried. But the worst was yet to come.

When Rik was 18, the Khmer Rouge took control of Cambodia. On that dreaded day, the village chief notified the villagers that they were to kill the animals they owned so there would be food to eat. The villagers were told that they were going to be moved from their village to another place, though they didn't know where.

The village chief gathered his community together and announced that if there were any people who worked for the government or who were educated, they were to notify him, so they could welcome the King to Siem Reap. Those villagers went and registered, and so did some uneducated farmers who lied, as they wanted to grasp this opportunity to meet the King. They were taken away and executed. The story about meeting the King had been a lie. This was year zero, and all educated citizens or people who worked for the government were deemed not to be trusted.

A couple of days later, after having been left in the dark, uncertain of their future, Rik's family were told they were going to be moved to Krobei Riel, a commune approximately 8km from their home. It was communicated that they needed to prepare rice to eat on the journey; however, as they would be returning in one week, they didn't need to take much. Rik and her family packed their rice, vegetables, and cooking utensils in bamboo baskets and carried them with sticks over their shoulders. With their cow in tow, they started the journey to Krobei Riel by foot.

With thousands of people making the journey, it took a week to walk 8km, under the guidance of one soldier. At that time, there weren't roads to walk on; only farms to navigate through. As the sun set each evening, Rik's family and thousands of other people would settle down for the night. Many people died along the way due to illnesses and were buried by their families. Pregnant women gave birth with no support, as the doctors and nurses had already been slaughtered by the soldiers.

When they finally reached Krobei Riel, all the families who survived the journey were instructed to build small houses. Without any materials, they had to forage the forests to find bamboo and palm leaves. The families worked together to build the houses one by one, staying in the abandoned local school whilst the work was being completed.

Once the houses were finished being built, a meeting was called by the soldiers, as there were more by that time. The villagers were divided into 'categories' according to their level of education and skills. Rik, having studied until grade six, was allocated to be teacher for the children. Her youngest brother was too young to contribute to the community, so he was permitted to stay at home. Rik's sister, who had been in primary school at the time, was responsible for carrying fertiliser to the farms, cutting small trees, and making compost. As her father was a woodworker, his job was to make cow carts and other wood items. The villagers without an education or skill were forced to perform hard labour in the farms and rice fields.

To stamp out any memories of the 'old way', the local school was destroyed, and a new school was built from bamboo. When teaching, Rik used a dry candle to draw Khmer letters and numbers on the chalkboard, as she didn't have access to chalk. She taught children who were aged between six and 15 each day. Some students learnt for half a day, then worked the other half of the day. Those who were 14 or 15 often had to skip school so they could help with transporting fertiliser.

The newly formed community was ruled by a handful of soldiers who carried guns and wore bandoliers over their shoulders to remind people of their power. They enforced an endless number of rules that came from a higher power. Adults and teenage boys and girls could not make eye contact or speak with each other. They could only eat the food that was provided. If the farmers were told to plant a certain amount of rice a day, they had to finish it. If they were told to do something, they had to do it in a certain amount of time. However, if they finished too quickly, their quota would be increased the next day. People mostly worked from 6am in the morning until 9pm at night.

If the rules were broken, a meeting would be held in the community, and the soldiers would encourage the 'rule breaker' to fix their problem. However, if the problem persisted, such as the person taking food from another source, their whole family would be slaughtered as a result. Their hands would be tied with string and attached to a bicycle, whilst the soldier rode the bicycle, leaving the unfortunate villager to run after it for the whole 8km journey to a pagoda that had been turned into a prison. They were then killed.

Although the community members never had enough to eat, and many died from malnutrition and starvation, Rik was lucky. The soldiers trusted her, so they gave her extra food that she was permitted to share with her father and siblings.

Rik is haunted daily by the memory of a starving family who had recently been moved from Banteay Meanchey, a province over 100km from Siem Reap. The soldiers were often making families move from one province to another, and this family had been deprived of food for so long that they didn't have energy to do anything. The mother in the family had sourced a small piece of sugarcane, which she was sucking on for energy. Despite her children reaching up to grab it, she made the difficult decision not to share it with them, as she knew she needed it for her survival. It wasn't enough though, and she died of starvation soon after, with all three of her children following her just a few days later. This was the new Cambodia, and that meant dozens of people were dying in Rik's community each week. The neighbours were responsible for burying the victims.

Pol Pot, the leader of the Democratic Republic of Kumpuchea (nowadays known as Cambodia), wanted all citizens to be the same. Everyone had to wear a black uniform, which would be replaced every few months if they were 'good'. With the majority of the educated having been murdered, there were no doctors to take care of sick villagers. Instead, this responsibility fell on a soldier with no medical background. To 'treat' his patients, he would inject coconut juice into their arms with a syringe.

The community members were forced to move around a lot, particularly when construction was required in other places, or there was rice that needed harvesting. Since Rik was a teacher, she would have to leave her family for weeks at a time to teach the children in rice fields. They had to walk to every destination, which took a toll on the villagers and resulted in further deaths.

In 1978, three years after Cambodia had been overthrown, Rik's father remarried. His new wife, who was just a couple of years older than Rik, was ill-tempered. One day, she argued with one of the leaders in the village, which put a black mark on her family. Determined to save her family from execution, Rik asked another leader who trusted her if her family could be moved back to the village where they had lived before the Khmer Rouge took power. She was granted permission on the condition that she would be paired off for marriage, as at the age of 20, it wasn't socially acceptable for her to be living as a single

IT'S NOT ABOUT ME

woman anymore. With her family being her only priority, Rik agreed.

There were 47 other couples who were paired off on the day Rik married her husband. They were taken to the pagoda and sat on the ground while soldiers called the names of each couple and asked them to stand up. They told the couples, 'You are married from today,' and that was it. Although most people were paired up by the soldiers, Rik's husband was allowed to choose her. His boss had heard about her and recommended Rik, telling her husband she was a good girl. Rik never loved her husband.

Two weeks after they were married, the Khmer Rouge was overthrown. Rik had known about this in advance, as the leader in her village had a radio notifying her that the Vietnamese were invading. That same leader offered Rik a big amount of gold, however, she refused as she thought the leader was testing her so she could kill her. The soldiers who supported Pol Pot fled because they were afraid they would be killed.

Rik's family walked from their village to where she was living. This time, it only took them a few hours because they were so happy to be free.

Rik lived with her husband's friend in their village. As it was rice harvesting season, they fortunately had enough rice to eat. There were ample vegetables and many fish to catch in the rice field. As the houses in the village had been destroyed during the Khmer Rouge, they were free to take what land they wanted. Rik and her husband claimed land at Penechey

Village, not far from where Rik had grown up. The provincial leader had offered her land in town, but as she thought it was haunted, she said no. That man died of a gunshot wound to his head a couple of months after the Khmer Rouge fell. He had been accused of corruption; some people say he committed suicide; others say he was murdered. Like many deaths that happened during the regime, people will never know the truth.

Rik had a very difficult life with her husband. After the Khmer Rouge regime fell, it was incredibly challenging for him to earn money. Originally, his work sent him to Palin, a rural province, to sell ox, however he was robbed along the way and lost everything. This shattered his confidence, and he turned to drinking and gambling. He became an alcoholic and, when Rik didn't agree with him, he would verbally abuse her. Rik and her husband had eight children together, and to raise them, her husband fished and harvested rice, which Rik would then sell at the market. When Rik's children were naughty or played too much, her husband would hit them on the back with bamboo sticks and often verbally abused them too. Rik's husband has now stopped drinking, they still don't have a happy marriage, as she can't forget the past. Although she has no love for him, they still live in the same house, for the sake of their children.

Rik's family and friends don't speak about their experiences during the Khmer Rouge. Although she feels happy that Cambodia has been slowly healing, Rik constantly worries that these atrocities will happen again in the future.

THORNG THOEUN WAS BORN into a poor family in Bakong District, about 17km from the centre of Siem Reap. His family lived in a house made from palm leaves and bamboo. When he was young, Thorng studied at the primary school at the local pagoda. The oldest of eight children, he had to stop studying in grade six as his family couldn't afford it.

With no employment opportunities in the countryside, Thorng took care of his family's farm. As time went by, the fighting between the Khmer Rouge and the Lon Nol government intensified. As the Khmer Rouge were the more powerful party in Thorng's village, he was told that he had to sign up to fight for what they called 'the red army'. If he didn't sign up to be a soldier, the Khmer Rouge were going to send his parents far away from their hometown. Wanting to avoid this, Thorng enlisted to fight for the Khmer Rouge. He then ran away from his home to instead fight with Lon Nol's army.

Thorng spent six months training in Siem Reap, learning the strategies of fighting, shooting rifles, using grenades, bombs and other weapons. He was willing to fight for Lon Nol as he knew the Khmer Rouge were committing unimaginable acts and that a big war would occur if they took power.

Thorng's team travelled all around Cambodia to fight the Khmer Rouge soldiers. At one point in time, whilst in Battambang, Pol Pot's soldiers surrounded them for seven days and nights. A plane from their side dropped parachutes with bombs towards them, however, they only managed to receive three bombs, with the enemy capturing the rest. Thorng's leader encouraged his team to fight the other side and push them out. Although they were successful, fifteen people from Thorng's team died that day.

When Thorng was 21, the Khmer Rouge took control of Cambodia. His team heard through the radio communication that Phnom Penh had fallen, and the government had lost. They were told to put down their weapons and not fight back.

The Khmer Rouge soldiers came to Thorng's barracks and took down the names of all the soldiers who resided there. They were then taken in a truck to Bakong district, close to his hometown, to be killed. On the first night, the Khmer Rouge soldiers executed the generals of Thorng's group. Knowing they would be killed on the second night, Thorng's team of 20 made a plan, which, if successful, would see them escape.

Luck was on their side, as there was a big thunderstorm that evening, so the security guard who was responsible for staying at the gate to the compound had moved elsewhere to seek shelter. When the coast was clear, they escaped one by one, with Thorng being the leader. They reached Thorng's village

IT'S NOT ABOUT ME

and rested there for one night, then started the long walk back to Siem Reap. As there were not enough soldiers to spend the time to catch them, the journey was relatively safe.

The team ended up in Kok Krosaing village, the hometown of some of their team members. Luck continued to be on Thorng's side, as the soldier that Pol Pot had sent to manage the village was his friend from the monkhood. Despite being a soldier for the enemy, his friend removed Thorng's and the team member's names from the register so that they weren't marked for death. Thorng ended up staying with his friend and a woman who was a mother-figure to him.

Thorng's job was to measure the rice fields and allocate work for people to do. He made sure he allocated the same amount to everyone so that it wasn't unfair, though he didn't pity the people who had to work in the rice fields, as he knew it was the rule and couldn't be changed. Thorng would remind the villagers not to work too quickly, otherwise their daily quota would be increased.

When the villagers didn't finish their work on time, Thorng made reasons for them to the leaders so they wouldn't be punished. Thorng recounts that his leaders weren't as brutal as leaders in other parts of Cambodia, so they accepted his reasons. Fortunately, Thorng never had to send anyone to their death.

For a while, Thorng moved near Phnom Kroam, a mountain about 8km from his village. There were people there digging roads and cutting small trees, so he had to monitor them. While there, Thorng fell in love with a girl and would show her favour with giving her less work. Though others found out, due to his position and friendship with one of the leaders, he didn't get into trouble.

Even as a person who was responsible for monitoring others, Thorng had to follow the rules. If he had broken them, he would have been taken to the pagoda and, as he recounts, hit in the head with a piece of wood until he died.

The memory that sticks out most horrifically in his mind was when a man in Thorng's village was taken to the prison at the pagoda because people branded him a bad man. If somebody didn't like another person, they could just say they were bad; then they were taken away. Thorng went to the pagoda to plead for the man's life, but when he got there, nothing could be done. They tied the man's hands and used black fabric to cover his eyes. He begged for his life, and said, 'Please don't kill me or hurt me,' but they didn't listen. Thorng said the soldiers used an axe to hit his head numerous times until he stopped breathing.

Although many people didn't have enough food to eat, Thorng did thanks to his friendship with the leader. He could save some food to give to others, but he had to hide it. He couldn't let the leader or other people see it, or he would be punished.

Towards the end of 1978, Thorng decided he wanted to get married. His trusted friend told him about a young woman named Rik who had a good reputation in the community. Love began to swell in his heart, and he asked for them to be married. Little did he know, Rik would never feel love for him.

On the day the Khmer Rouge ended, Thorng saw Pol Pot's soldiers run away. His friend collected the weapons in the village and gave them to the good soldiers. Thorng then walked to his homeland to find his family. Although his parents were alive, two of his siblings had died from illnesses. Another one of his brothers was missing and presumed dead. In 1988, they found out that his brother had survived. He had been near the Thai border when the Khmer Rouge fell and managed to get on a plane and move to Canada. His wife was looking for Thorng's family and sent some money. Feeling so lucky, Thorng named his son who was born that year, 'Dollar'.

Now in his sixties, Thorng takes care of his buffalos and cows every day. He tries to put the travesties to the back of his mind, but he still remembers so much from that time. He hopes it will never happen again, but he isn't certain.

THE PAGODA WHERE THORNG and Rik were forcefully married is where our organisation was originally located. It fathoms me how Rik, Thorng, and other survivors can drive past the pagoda every day without getting pulled into the past. That's the thing though; they just had to get on with life. They had no other choice.

SALLY HETHERINGTON OAM

When things feel overwhelming, and I wonder how I can move past situations, I think of Rik, Thorng, and all the other Cambodians who survived the Khmer Rouge. They had to overcome so much to rebuild their lives from nothing and, although they mightn't think so, they are stronger because of it.

4. Discovering the Key to Sustainability

WHEN I BECAME INVOLVED with Human Hopes Association, we really were starting from scratch. Although Human Hopes Association had been running for a year and a half when I joined, and the Khmer volunteers were trying hard, they had lacked the time, money, resources, and experience to really make something out of the association. That is where I came in. Since this was my full-time job, I could commit countless hours, in and out of the office, to developing the school and the team.

Before we could get started, we needed to address a pressing issue. The monks at the pagoda we were based at had complained that our students were being noisy and disrupting their peace. They had given us an ultimatum: make the place much quieter, or we were not permitted to stay there any longer. We held a meeting in one of our large upstairs classrooms, and with all the monks at the pagoda attending, along with the pagoda committee, we attempted to keep the peace and ensure we could remain at this location. I was cautious, as the previous organisation that had been based at this pagoda expressed they had experienced issues with the monks. However, without me understanding a word that was said, we reached a verbal agreement that we could continue to stay at the pagoda as long as we reduced the noise from our students.

After this was sorted, the first thing we did was update the name of our organisation. Although it stayed the same in Khmer, the English version was changed to 'Human and Hope Association', just to make it a bit easier. I know that it isn't the most attractive name, and many people have told me since then that we should change it, but we aren't going to. That is the name that the Cambodians who founded the organisation chose, and I respect that. The name apparently has a good meaning in Khmer. *Samakom monu ning kdei sangkum* is how you would pronounce it in English, but if you meet a Khmer person, ask them to say it for you as my English translation of the Khmer Sanskrit could use some improvement.

Next up was creating a comfortable learning environment for our students. We needed to revamp the office and create a dedicated library. The issue was, we didn't have any money. Like I have always said, things have a way of working out, and on one October day in 2012, a friend of mine randomly sent me AUD$1,000 through PayPal to do with whatever we pleased. We used this money to paint a classroom, hire a local builder to create a bookshelf and table, and purchase books for our new library. I sure do miss those days when the exchange rate was dollar for dollar!

Together, our team of Khmer volunteers plus some of the young adult students from the school I previously worked at, spent a weekend scraping, fixing, painting the walls, and doing a big clean out. We installed new whiteboards in the classrooms to replace the yellow, peeling boards that the teachers were struggling to write on. We purchased three new desks for the office; one for me, one for the director, and one for the Khmer volunteers to share. We sold the bulky computers that had long seen their use-by date and purchased two laptops. And, for my nagging back pain, we bought two padded office chairs to replace the splintering, red plastic chairs the team had been sitting on for far too long.

We had one squat toilet for 300 students, and that toilet happened to have a broken door and roof with holes in it that you could see into from the second storey of our school. Using a squat toilet after you have drunk bad water is difficult enough, try using it knowing that everyone could see in! A former student came and replaced the door and roof and, for good measure, also installed a light so we wouldn't have to do our business in the dark anymore. The initial AUD$1,000 went a long way to improving the condition of our school, but the fact was, we needed money to pay rent to the monks, keep the electricity on, and eventually get a salary for our team of volunteers.

Before all that could happen, we were required to register as an NGO with the ministry in Cambodia. This was a process I knew nothing about, but fortunately, the director and one of our volunteers who worked in the local commune office took the task on. I put a call out to my friends, and one of them donated the estimated fee we figured we would need for the registration. Technically, registering an organisation in Cambodia should be free. However, as it is a notoriously corrupt country (Cambodia is currently ranked the 161 least corrupt nation out of 175 countries)[v], we had to pay money to every person involved at every step along the way. First, a document needed to be made by our team to suit the requirements of the ministry. This happened without the input of most of our team, and I wish we had been involved, as it caused unwanted stress for our team later down the track. In this document, we needed to explain our governance, our projects, and what we were aiming to achieve. As we were very young, we hadn't worked all of this out yet, so the document didn't truly reflect what we were doing. Our director and volunteer went to the village chief, the commune chief, the provincial chief, and then the document eventually made its way to Phnom Penh, where it reached the ministry. In the end, the process cost us USD$850, leaving us with some leftover cash in the coffers. To this day, the fact that we had to pay such an enormous fee in order to help the community really doesn't sit well with me.

It was then time to stop the foreign volunteering. Although it took some words of encouragement, the director agreed that we should stop accepting foreign teaching volunteers. My case for support was that if we ran workshops for our Khmer volunteers, they would have the necessary skills to ensure the best outcomes for their students. We decided that if foreign volunteers with unique skills approached us, we would consider working with them. When it came to English teaching, we could definitely provide an environment that empowered the local team to aim high. I had learnt my lessons from my time at the other organisation, and I didn't want to repeat those mistakes.

It was then time to get serious about what we were going to do to help the community. Although we were teaching English, 'morality', and Buddhist studies, I knew that there was so much more we could do to help break the cycle of poverty in our community. We needed projects with quick outcomes, and not just those based around children and young adults. We then came up with our mission: to empower Cambodians to create a sustainable future for themselves through projects focused on education, community development and vocational training. From our mission then came the five core values.

A family of six children who attended Human and Hope Association.

Empowerment – we aim to empower people to create long-term change for themselves, and our community.

Sustainability – we believe in the importance of ensuring that positive change is long-lasting and intergenerational; a long-term solution to poverty.

Equality – we do not discriminate on any basis, including age, gender or social status. We believe everyone is deserving of opportunities and support.

Integrity – we believe in doing what is right even when it is difficult and hope to promote this value to our students and community.

Transformation – we hope to foster positive growth for individuals as well as promote social change in our community and Cambodia generally.

And finally, to keep us focused, our aims:
1. To provide free services to Level One and Two beneficiaries so education and vocational opportunities are available to all members of our community.
2. To provide quality education to our students by capacity building our staff.
3. To promote strong, united families where children have access to education and parents have the skills to find sustainable employment.
4. To teach morality and values subjects to students as part of a holistic approach to education and community development.
5. To create long-term, positive change by addressing the underlying causes of poverty and disadvantage and implementing projects to tackle these causes.

Our first new project that the team unanimously decided on was providing hygiene workshops to the students. With help from another NGO who already had the resources prepared, we gathered the students on a cold Sunday in December and explained the importance of hand washing and teeth brushing in a fun and informative way. With diarrhoeal diseases accounting for approximately 10,000 deaths a year in Cambodia each year[vi], we knew that poor hygiene practices were something we could address in a short period of time. We provided each student with a bar of soap, a toothbrush, and toothpaste, and encouraged them to utilise their knowledge at home. To ensure that their habits were maintained, we determined that we would hold these workshops every six months, a commitment that has been maintained to this day. We also provided the students with individual water bottles, however, they went unused, and were eventually discarded, as the students took a preference to their communal drinking cups.

DEVELOPING A SOURCE OF funding for Human and Hope Association was no easy task. It was hanging over my head that I would need an income to support myself, as I had been ploughing through my savings and relying on the generosity of family and friends. We also needed funding to promote some of the Khmer volunteers to permanent employees. In January 2013, I received an email from a man who, on behalf of a couple from Europe, was looking for an organisation to support in Cambodia. I thought it was going to be our lucky break. This man and I spoke on the phone, and I gave him a pitch about what Human and Hope Association did, and what we wished to achieve. He then surprised me. The couple from Europe were actually looking for an organisation that they could 'own' and be called the directors of. I cut the man off, telling him that Human and Hope Association wasn't looking for someone to 'own' the organisation. We were

IT'S NOT ABOUT ME

all about ensuring the local team felt empowered to take charge, and that even I would be leaving the organisation in the future. We didn't want funds with those sorts of conditions attached to them. That situation was a great lesson for me; it was the beginning of learning to say 'no' to donors, a skill that served me well down the track.

The issue was, we still needed cash. As Cambodia was a blacklisted country with PayPal, and transfer fees would cost more than the donations themselves, the only way we could get money from my Australian friends was to have them deposit money into my Australian bank account, which I would then give to Human and Hope Association out of the funds I was holding in Cambodia. Although this wasn't ideal, and to be honest, I can't believe so many people trusted me to do that, it helped us get off the ground. To start with, friends and family gave ten dollars here, and twenty dollars there. It allowed us to purchase the necessities, but we weren't any closer to sourcing salaries.

Fortunately, a couple of months down the track, I secured a monthly donation from an overseas donor with a strong interest in Cambodia. Her USD$500 a month was transferred into my personal account in Cambodia, as we couldn't set up our own bank account until we were registered as an NGO. With these funds, we were able to pay my monthly salary of USD$100, and although it didn't cover my rent, it did bring me a small amount of financial relief. The director received a salary of USD$150 a month, and we were then able to pay our volunteers a stipend of USD$0.50 per one-hour lesson taught. The remaining funds paid for our internet, rent, electricity, and study supplies. Finally, we were on our way!

LOSING FACE IS A dominate aspect of the culture in Cambodia. People don't like to be humiliated (I mean, who does?), and if they are nice humans, they will try not to let others lose face, either. It was this culture that resulted in us accepting two French volunteers at Human and Hope Association, even after we had cancelled our foreign teaching volunteer program.

I came to work one day in January 2013, and our director at the time said to me, 'Sally, we will have two volunteers to teach here for the next four days.'

'*What?!*' I exclaimed. 'We have cancelled the foreign volunteer program. How did this happen?'

'Yesterday, after you had left work, a tour guide brought two French tourists to Human and Hope Association. He had already told them they could volunteer, because he used to bring tourists here. I couldn't say no, because then he would lose face in front of the tourists,' the director replied.

I was exasperated, but there was nothing I could do. That evening the two young French men came to Human and Hope Association, much to my reluctance. After speaking with them for a few minutes, it was obvious that they only had a basic grasp of the English language. On the second evening of teaching, one of the men came to me and told me that they wouldn't be returning. They realised they didn't have the skills for it.

Although I was relieved that they came to that conclusion on their own, I couldn't shake the feeling of annoyance. The situation left me even more determined to show the world that locally-run organisations were the best thing for local communities.

ABOUT A MONTH AFTER the encounter with the French volunteers, I began running child protection workshops. We had implemented our visitor policy, which only allowed visitors to come to Human and Hope Association with appointments, provided they adhered to our strict conditions. We had erected a sign at the pagoda: 'No visitors without appointments, and no photos or videos'. We were determined to keep tourists away unless they had an appointment.

The first step of the child protection workshop was to educate our staff and Khmer volunteers on why child protection was important, the different types of abuse, and how we could keep our students safe in their communities and at Human and Hope Association. The second part was to teach them how to appropriately interact with tourists who came to visit the pagoda and as a result would come across Human and Hope Association. If you have ever visited Cambodia, you would know that Khmer people are known for their friendliness and that they go out of their way to accommodate a request even though it may be against the rules. They don't want to lose face, and they don't want the other person to lose face either. We practiced what they could say to these tourists, being polite but firm, and made a video of it. It took quite some time, but after a couple of hours our team were able to confidently tell me (the 'tourist') in English that I wasn't allowed to come and visit Human and Hope Association without an appointment, nor was I allowed to take photos of the children. They are not zoo animals, nor are they tourist attractions.

A few days later when I arrived at work, my colleague told me a story of something that had happened the previous day.

'Sally, a lady from Portugal came to Human and Hope Association yesterday. She walked into a teacher's classroom while he was teaching and told him that she wanted to teach the children a song in Portuguese.'

'Are you serious? And what did he do?' I responded, my heart racing.

'The teacher tried to tell her that she had to leave, but she wouldn't listen. She said she could help. But the teacher's English isn't so good, so he took her out of the classroom and got me. I tried to tell her that she cannot come and teach the students and that it was against our rules. She still wouldn't listen to me. So, I told her to come to the front of the building with me. When we got to the sign, I pointed at it angrily and told her, 'You must go'. She looked annoyed, then she left. I was so angry because she wouldn't listen to me.'

'That's fine,' I told him. 'I understand why you got angry. I am proud of you for telling her to go away.'

That story is usually the first one I tell people when I speak out against poverty tourism and voluntourism. I always pose the question: who turns up at a school and demands to interrupt a class to teach children a song? If you did that in Australia, you would most likely be kicked out of the school and the police would be called. However, things like this happen *all the time* in Cambodia. It certainly wasn't to be the last time a tourist tried to walk into a classroom at Human and Hope Association.

5. The Unfair Treatment of Women

MOVING TO CAMBODIA HAD been a cultural shock for me, but the biggest change was seeing the way women were treated. A popular proverb in Cambodia is 'men are gold and women are cloth, the former easily cleaned, the latter easily stained.' Until 2007, 'chbab srey' (roughly translated to 'female code of conduct') was taught in schools in Cambodia.[vii] Girls learnt that they had to be respectful to their husbands and were told not to take personal problems away from home.

Women are born with a lesser status than men in Cambodian culture, which is why we established the sewing program at Human and Hope Association, to begin to address gender inequality within the community. While gender inequality exists in Australia, it was so much more overt and apparent in Cambodia, where men dictated whether their wives or daughters could work or pursue an education. As a female living in Australia, this really opened my eyes to the realities outside of home, which only made me more determined to somehow provide women with the right tools and an environment to feel empowered, where we could start a movement that would affect future generations.

The sewing program aims to change the opinions of the rural poor that educating females is a waste of time. An opinion we often face when recruiting students for the program is that being a caretaker is a woman's priority, and there is no need in their lives for education. With a lack of education and poverty comes a lack of confidence, with many having to rely on their husbands to survive. We identified that this created further power imbalances and a reliance on their spouses. By providing our students with a skill, they can earn an income and pave the way to financial independence. One of our students had previously separated from her husband, however, realising she couldn't survive financially without him, she returned to the difficult marriage. After she borrowed funds for a sewing machine through our microfinance program, she felt that she didn't have to be attached to her husband to survive, and this time she left him permanently, confident in her ability to look after herself and her son. I did a fist punch in the air, 'The Breakfast Club' style, when I heard that.

I had initially moved to Cambodia with the urge to help children, but over time, I realised that by helping their mothers earn an income and feel confident and strong, we could help children at the same time. The women who graduate from our sewing program have developed into respected role models for our community. They set good examples for their children, who are then enrolled in our education programs and remain long after their mothers finish studying. By showing our community that women are capable of so much more than being caretakers, who can set up their own businesses or earn a sustainable income, they are challenging gender stereotypes and making our community a safer place for girls to fulfil their dreams and break the cycle of poverty.

I ONCE ASKED MY friend how he managed to have sex with his wife when they only had one bed, which his young son also slept on.

'When my son falls asleep at night, I carefully push him to the end of the bed, then I have sex with my wife,' he answered, making me wish I had never asked the question.

I also asked this friend if he slept with sex workers. He darted his eyes from side to side, bowed his head, and answered yes. I asked him why. He told me it was out of respect for his wife; he didn't want to ask her for sex very often, so he visited sex workers with his friends. It cost USD$5 per visit. I asked him if his wife knew about his visit to the brothels. He said yes, as he couldn't bear lying to her. I asked him how that made her feel. He bowed his head again. He said it made her feel sad.

In a study on Cambodian men who have sex, researchers interviewed 133 Cambodian men who visited brothels on a regular basis. It was revealed that 83% of sex buyers currently had a wife or girlfriend.

More than half (56%) of the men had 26 or more sexual partners during their lifetimes.[viii] Yet, if a woman has more than one sexual partner, she is considered impure and a 'bad girl'.

Karaoke bars are a hotbed for paid sexual activity. Although I mainly visited small, seemingly legitimate karaoke bars during my time in Cambodia, I once visited a three-storey karaoke parlour that had an array of women waiting to be 'picked' by those visiting. These women dress in what Cambodians classify as revealing clothing and sit on a row of seats. During the evening, they are called into different karaoke rooms, where they play companion to the intoxicated men inside. What goes on after that, I'm sure you can figure out.

When I visited this karaoke parlour, I felt downcast about the situation the 'karaoke women' were in. They were put on show like animals in a pet store, waiting to be plucked out based on their appearances and displays of affection. I had no idea if they were ever put in dangerous situations, though men tend to dehumanise sex workers (or karaoke women) and use that detachment to act out their fantasies. According to the previously mentioned survey, 89% of buyers viewed sex workers as fundamentally different from other women. 98% of buyers made harsh, negative judgments about women in prostitution. What became apparent in the survey was that the men demand these behaviours from women who turn to sex work and simultaneously denigrate them for it.

When I mentioned my concerns about the wellbeing of the karaoke women to my friend, she explained to me that she had previously interviewed women at this parlour. She told me that the women she interviewed as part of her job were all in unhappy marriages, and that this work was an escape for them. Their husbands didn't care that they were doing the work, they were just interested in receiving the money that came from it. I just hope that these women feel empowered and safe in their jobs, as every human being deserves to be.

THERE WAS A STUDENT who would always come to Human and Hope Association a couple of hours early each day and just wait on the balcony. She was around eight years old and was always eager to chat with the staff. Even when we moved to our new community centre, her grandmother would put her on the back of her bicycle and bring her to and from Human and Hope Association every day. She would bring her lunch in a container and eat near the team, always keen to have a conversation. I will never forget a story she told a teacher one day when she came to school.

'Teacher, today a lady in my village was killed by her husband. He asked her to borrow a chicken from a neighbour, but she didn't want to, as she was ashamed. He took an axe and killed her with it. Then I went and saw the body. He is now in gaol, and his son doesn't have parents.'

She said this as though it was a normal, everyday occurrence.

When I listened to my colleague translate the story, I didn't feel shock. Instead, I felt a sadness for the people of Cambodia. There is so much violence in the country, particularly aimed at women, and children are growing up used to it. That is dangerous pattern to fall into. It is something that, no matter what the culture dictates, we shouldn't be accepting.

A UNITED NATIONS REPORT RELEASED in 2013 showed that 1 in 5 men in Cambodia between the ages of 18-49 had admitted to raping a woman.[ix] Although rape is a crime in Cambodia, many victims are scared to report it. This could be due to a lack of evidence and medical support, fear of retaliation from the perpetrator, lack of confidence in the justice system, or a fear of being branded for life as a 'non-virgin' in the community. Cambodia places a high value on women's virginity, so they are often shamed for being the victim of sexual assault and rape, which makes those girls unmarriageable in the eyes of those in the community.

In 2012 a good friend of mine was raped in Cambodia; the perpetrator faced no consequences for his actions. Angered by this decision, I was determined to contribute to increasing the awareness of Cambodian women's rights through their knowledge and confidence and help them find the courage to fight back against what seemed so 'normal' in their society. I held workshops at Human and Hope Association, explaining the meaning of consent, giving startling statistics about sexual abuse in Cambodia, and encouraging them to contact the police if they saw something or if something happened to them.

A couple of months later, a workshop participant experienced an attempted rape against her at her home. Fortunately, she fought back against this abusive man, but it really shook her up. Instead of just accepting this attempted rape, something incredible happened. This brave, young woman decided that it was not okay. Informed by the workshops we had held, she received the support of her mother and she stood up for her rights. I organised for her to stay in a safe guesthouse for a couple of nights, and she contacted the local police to report the perpetrator.

The police did nothing.

They told her that if she could ask the perpetrator to come to the police station, they would educate him on why he shouldn't rape people. Which of course, wasn't going to happen. The perpetrator left town, and although scarred, this brave woman moved on with her life.

Because justice is often not served in sexual assault and rape cases, victims aren't willing to come forward. Unless a big spotlight is shone on this issue, and major reforms are taken to address the high rape statistics, this issue of gender inequality and the existing power imbalances in Cambodia will only continue, if not, worsen.

IT'S NOT ABOUT ME

MOST OF MY CAMBODIAN FRIENDS have suffered violence in their families, regardless of whether they are male or female. I also was a victim of violence while in Cambodia; something that, although encouraged to be quiet about, I was encouraged to speak out about.

Prior to working at Human and Hope Association, I was a weekly volunteer at an English school near Angkor Wat. I had promised to commit a minimum of a year to their program, so I could teach conversational English from a workbook I had created and provide training to the local staff. I was invited to their staff retreat in January 2013, where my colleague, who I had developed a close relationship with, showed his true colours on that trip. On the long bus ride to Sihanoukville, he drank a dozen cans of beer, and used the alcohol as an excuse to push me hard – twice. The next day, he and his colleagues continued the bender, and this man punched me in the arm and grabbed my neck, causing injuries that lasted a couple of days. With it apparent that this wasn't a big deal to the man or his colleagues that watched on, I fled back to Siem Reap thanks to the financial and emotional support of a friend in Australia. The perpetrator contacted me after I made a complaint about him and told me that what went on was nobody's business but ours (I later learnt this is a common belief in Cambodia), and that I had no right to complain about him.

I wrote a letter to the director of the organisation that wasn't taken seriously. His deputy came to Human and Hope Association, and despite me saying I wanted my colleague in the room who knew of the situation, he wanted to speak privately. He proceeded to tell me that the director was so stressed over the situation, and that he hated to see his director unhappy. I told him I didn't care that my complaint had made the director stressed; one of his staff members had acted violently towards me while everyone else looked on. Although many women would stay quiet about it out of fear of persecution, I wasn't going to take this standing down. It was my responsibility to speak up, in the hopes that violence against other women would be prevented in the future. Instead, I was made to feel ashamed, a feeling that still resonates with me to this day when I hear stories about what a 'good guy' so and so was before he murdered his wife. There is so much to be done, not just in Cambodia, but worldwide, about how victims of violence are treated. Unfortunately, nothing came out of the conversation. The issue was swept under the rug, and I cut ties with the organisation and perpetrator.

6. Direct Aid and False Promises

'**TEN POSTCARDS FOR ONE** dollar. One, two, three, four, five, six, seven, eight, nine, ten.' The young girl at Ta Prohm temple showed the postcards she was holding to the tourist waiting in the tuk-tuk beside her.

'No,' he answered.

'I need money, you buy 10 for one dollar,' she persisted.

The man kept saying no. The girl stayed firmly planted. Finally, the man gave in.

'If I give you one dollar, will you leave me alone?'

Watching all this unfold from the comfort of the tuk-tuk I was sitting in, I finally decided to say something. 'It isn't a good idea to buy from that child or give her money,' I called out.

The guy looked over at me and responded, 'I know, but she is so annoying, I just want to get rid of her.'

'That's her strategy,' I replied. 'However, stand your ground. If you give her that dollar, you're just perpetuating the problem and she'll just continue begging on the streets her whole life.'

The man nodded and didn't reach for his wallet. Eventually, the girl walked away.

SALLY HETHERINGTON OAM

DO YOU GIVE TO children when you travel? I used to take pencils, coins, and lollies to low-income countries and give them to children I came across. I will never forget when I was ambushed at a temple in Myanmar in 2008 whilst giving out Australian five cent coins. I gave a coin to one child, and then dozens of other children rushed over. There was even an elderly man pleading with me for that tiny piece of copper that held such worth to them. I will never forget the scene that I inadvertently caused while trying to help. Years on, through reading case studies, talking to local people and seeing other tourists doing similar things, I have realised that this well-intentioned practice causes problems.

When we give lollies to children, it might seem like we are providing them with a little treat for the day. But didn't we grow up learning that we shouldn't accept candy from strangers? When we give candy and other trinkets to children, we are potentially opening them up to grooming. Call this far-fetched, but it happens. When you are giving presents to children, it makes them trust you, and then perhaps think that all strangers who give them presents are nice and without bad intentions. So, when the next person comes along and starts to groom a child, preparing to abuse or manipulate them, the child is more susceptible to trusting this person. It is far better to be extra cautious than too relaxed; you wouldn't think twice about protecting your children from stranger danger.

Giving can also cause resentment in communities. Think back to my story about the five cent coins. There were dozens of people, but only so many coins to give out. How was it fair that I gave to some, and not to others? If there are eleven children reaching out their hands to take a present from you, and you only have nine presents, what will happen to the other two children? How will they feel? There is a culture of 'losing face' in Asia, and I have known of community members who get extremely jealous when one child/family receives something, and they don't. It can cause conflict that will last long after you have departed in your tuk-tuk.

When you give to a child, they see the benefit then and there. An issue in Cambodia is that many people do not see the benefit of studying; they see the benefit of getting money immediately. So, when you give to a child, that child will put 2 + 2 together and see that if they are on the streets begging instead of in school, they will be able to support their families now; they won't care about the future when they are not 'young and cute' anymore and have no education to back them up.

A FEW YEARS AGO, I was at a hospital about 60km from Siem Reap, Cambodia. My friend, a nurse, was working as an advisor there to build the capacity of the nursing staff. She became frustrated as the staff weren't taking care of their equipment. When she raised the issue with them, they shrugged and responded, 'The foreign government will just give us more.'

Back in 2015, I was approached by an Australian charity who were doing work in Cambodia. They wanted feedback on the work they were undertaking. Basically, they would come over every couple of months, working with the local community in Siem Reap where they saw a need, and gave direct aid. They came armed with hundreds of kilograms of luggage, holding countless stuffed toys, shoes, clothing, and electronics, amongst other things. These items were distributed amongst families, students, teachers, and health centre workers. This is the feedback I gave them -it wasn't taken well.

Let's look at the clothing donation issue. When we give clothing for free to people in low-income countries, it undermines the local economy. Small, local businesses are affected as the recipients of the free clothing don't purchase new clothing from the local markets. Africa experienced a 50% reduction in apparel production between 1981 and 2000[x] due to the influx of clothing donations. This resulted in a decline in employment, which meant that citizens who didn't need assistance from aid programs before were more likely to rely on foreign donations because of the effects of said aid. Added to this, when we give clothing, it shifts the responsibility of providing for children and families from the parents/guardians to donors. It gives the wrong impression to the recipients, who begin to think that it is normal to receive handouts from foreigners, and they come to expect more of these donations. It shouldn't be normal, and local governments and NGOs need to be providing education and training opportunities to local people so that they can afford to buy clothing themselves, and not be shifting their basic responsibilities as parents onto someone else. This method isn't empowering, and it isn't creating long-term, sustainable change.

Then, there is the toys issue. Oh my, how many times I have seen charities distribute toys to children in Cambodia. But why? Why do children in Cambodia need toys? They are very versatile and can create their own games with no resources apart from their imagination. A favourite game the students at Human and Hope Association play involves their shoes and a lot of jumping. Yet, foreigners are distributing homemade stuffed animals made in their knitting circles as well as other toys because they *think* that is what Cambodian children need. It makes them, the donors, *feel* good. It makes them the hero of the story.

Supporting marginalised citizens is not about how it makes you feel. It is about what is best for the local people and communities, and to determine what is best for the local communities, you need input from the *local communities*. If you asked community leaders what they need to develop their society, they would not be saying 'stuffed animals'.

I ONCE WENT OUT to a rural community in Siem Reap with an NGO who was distributing donated goods. The villagers rushed to get close to the van that was filled to the brim with toys, shoes, clothing and stationery. It was chaos. I saw one woman who ended up taking ten pairs of shoes, without permission, and other villagers shoving each other to get their free goods. After everything was (unevenly) distributed, I took a walk down the road. To my disappointment, I saw a few toys that had been distributed to children lying on the side of the road, broken, and discarded.

When we give things for free, people don't tend to value them, as was the case of the nurses who worked at the rural hospital. This goes for many people, regardless of their wealth or status. I know that I personally respect and take care of things more when I have worked hard to purchase them myself. When you are given something, you don't connect that feeling of accomplishment and achievement with the item. Thus, there isn't a big willingness to protect those items, especially if the recipient is under the impression that there is 'plenty more where that came from'.

We once signed up a woman living in poverty to study in our sewing program at Human and Hope Association. However, just before the program began, a local NGO built her a house. After that she didn't want to study in the program where she could gain a skill that she could use to earn an income to support her children as a single mother. She already had a house given to her, so understandably, why would she need to enter into a program requiring hard work and commitment?

Some might argue that when we give direct aid, we are setting the recipients up for failure. I tend to agree with that. We are encouraging people to take aid instead of providing a platform for them to learn the skills and education they need to earn an income. It isn't a long-term solution, and in most cases, should only be used in emergency situations and disaster areas. Otherwise, it is putting a Band-Aid on the problem, more often or not to make the givers feel like they have done something useful.

DURING CHRISTMAS ONE YEAR, a tourist from Australia visited Siem Reap. At the last minute, he decided to give food, and put a call out on his social media for people to donate money to buy rice bags. He distributed these rice bags with the help of a translator who drove up to 'poor shacks' and asked the stories of the people living inside. He raised thousands of dollars and randomly gave these rice bags to handfuls of people.

I was asked by three different friends to approach this man and persuade him to direct his money elsewhere. I felt it was a hopeless case, however I reached out to him and explained what my Cambodian colleague thought about the situation. My colleague, Salin, who grew up in poverty himself, said that distributing the rice really creates a dependency for people. Even though to the donor it was a 'one off' donation, the mindset of many people is that when they receive something, they think it will always come, and they become dependent on it. Many don't have a willingness to work or seek income from other sources due to it.

The man didn't listen to my advice. Like many others before him, he attempted to justify his actions. He didn't see anything wrong with the fact that a stranger was going into people's houses and giving them rice. His message that this sort of giving was to be commended spread very far; I saw several people post about it and congratulate him on his actions. This was very concerning, as countless of other people would be believing that this is a great way of helping people and would be more likely to do it when they visit a low-income country in the future.

THERE USED TO BE a Khmer volunteer who taught at Human and Hope Association in addition to his full-time work teaching at a nearby NGO. The NGO he taught at was funded primarily by Australians who frequently visited the organisation. He formed a close relationship with a woman he called 'Mum'. One day in early 2013, this volunteer came into our office and proudly told me that his 'Mum' was going to pay for him to move to Australia to study. I was sceptical. I knew how difficult it was to get into Australia on a student visa, not to mention the costs associated with it. I had also grown used to foreigners visiting

IT'S NOT ABOUT ME

Cambodia and promising the people they met that they would help them. Most of the time, that was never the case.

Not wanting to discourage him, but at the same time, wanting him to understand the realities of the situation, I explained to him that he shouldn't get his hopes up too much. I gently told him that although I was sure his 'Mum' would try her best, it was difficult to get a visa into Australia. He nodded, but knowing he was someone who didn't often listen to the advice of others, I knew he didn't fully absorb what I said.

This volunteer told his community that he would be moving to Australia, and his girlfriend was beaming with pride that her boyfriend would be moving to this lucky country to get a better life. I cringed at the fact that he had already told the community, because knowing this wasn't going to end well, I had concerns for the volunteer losing face.

A few days after telling me the news, his 'Mum' emailed me. She told me that she had made a terrible mistake; she had promised her 'son' something she couldn't give him. When she made the offer, she hadn't properly thought out the mammoth effort, costs, and resources required to get our volunteer to Australia. Not prepared to tell this young man the truth, she asked that I explain to him that it wasn't going to happen. His dreams had looked like they were coming true, then a few days later, they were shattered.

I couldn't believe that this woman made such a huge mistake, then expected me to be the bearer of the bad news. As the let-down would be coming from me, not her, her relationship with her 'son' would most likely remain intact, whilst I would be the one to lose his trust and respect that I had been working so hard to build up.

That weekend, the director of Human and Hope Association and I called a meeting with the volunteer. I told the volunteer the truth; his 'Mum' had overpromised, and unfortunately, he wouldn't be able to move to Australia. He looked at me with the utmost sadness in his eyes, determined not to cry. I saw his heart break, and I knew that from that moment on our relationship would never be the same again. I had delivered the news that had caused his dreams to be taken away and him and his family to lose face in the community.

I didn't have any further contact with his 'Mum' after that. In my mind, she represents the countless foreigners who visit the traumatised country and promise things they just don't see through, not realising the devastating consequences their words can have.

FOR COMMUNITIES TO DEVELOP, there needs to be an investment in the local people. As humans, we often think that our goodwill is driven through the tangible and physical. This isn't the case; although you may not be able to physically feel a monetary donation, or see its influence, funding programs and local staff can be the most impactful support. Instead of giving out direct aid, please consider donating to a local organisation that has achieved successful outcomes in their community, and help them continue their great work.

SALLY HETHERINGTON OAM

7. Building up Human and Hope Association

WHEN I FIRST STARTED working at Human and Hope Association, I was required to teach one English class an evening due to a shortage of teachers. Every evening, between 5pm and 6pm, I would head to our library that doubled as a classroom, and teach seven young adult students, plus a monk who was eager to learn English from a native speaker.

The English language ability of the students varied, and I would often find myself running out of the classroom and bringing in a teacher from another class to help me translate my lessons. It wasn't efficient, nor was it sufficient quality for the students. After a few weeks, a Khmer man who had studied English Literature at university with a couple of our volunteers approached us, eager to help. We decided that he would take over my English class, and I could concentrate on doing what I did best - building up the organisation.

The director and I were working in the daytime, however, all our English classes were in the evenings, as our Khmer volunteers worked in other jobs or studied during the day. We knew the next step was to

IT'S NOT ABOUT ME

open up daytime classes for younger students, however, our volunteers weren't available in the daytime as they were at their paid jobs or studying in high school. I had proven that I wasn't suitable for the role. And the director, being a monk, would take two to three-hour lunch breaks and often had to spend time in the village attending ceremonies, so his presence at Human and Hope Association was inconsistent. It was time to promote one of our volunteers to paid employment.

One volunteer who had caught my eye was Heng*, a man who wouldn't even look me in the eye the first few times we met. He was an unusual character, very moody and not at all confident. However, I saw how hard he worked. He genuinely cared about our students and the quality of our education, so I knew he was somebody I could work with to develop. Heng worked full-time as a cleaner at a hotel, earning just USD$40 a month, plus tips. Although we couldn't pay him much, I worked out my budget, and decided we could afford to pay him USD$70 a month for full-time work, if he chose to accept our proposal.

The day the director and I sat down with Heng and offered him a role as a full-time English teacher was the defining moment in Human and Hope Association's development. This was us committing to enhancing the organisation and being prepared to make tough decisions. Heng was in disbelief when we offered him the role. He didn't believe he had the ability to take it on, and there was doubt in us choosing him over the other volunteers. With many words of support from myself and the director, he accepted the role.

With Heng, it was always two steps forward and one step back. Working on his confidence was one of the biggest challenges I faced in the first two and a half years at Human and Hope Association and sticking to his improvements was one of the biggest challenges Heng faced. When we first started the preschool program, which he was responsible for, an overwhelmed Heng asked me, 'How long will we do this for? Six months, then we can stop?'

And the next year, now a manager, I told Heng his communication hadn't been good the past few days, he said to me, 'Sally, next semester I don't want to be a manager anymore, I just want to be a teacher.' I told him, 'No. I do *not* accept that. I know that you are just afraid of not doing a good job. I give you some feedback and you decide to give up? Heng, you *are* doing an amazing job. And you *can* continue to improve. Heng, repeat after me, "I can, I can, I can".' A few months later, when I was incredibly stressed, he sent me a text message saying, 'One week ago I saw your face is not happy. How can I help you? I support you everything. I think that you are so clever to take care of yourself and solve the problem. I trust in you. You can, you can, you can!' And you know what? His text message worked. I snapped out of my stress after that.

IT'S NOT ABOUT ME

ABOUT A WEEK AFTER we promoted Heng to full-time employment, one of our volunteers, Chan*, came to the director and I and asked us for help. He had been working at the local commune office, earning a measly salary each month, however, he hadn't been paid in three months. He needed money, or he wouldn't be able to finish his university degree.

Chan was a timid man who appeared to follow instead of lead. His English language skills were at an elementary level; however, he had come to us for help, and knowing he had the respect of his students, we wanted to support him.

I reached out to friends and was able to secure donations that would enable us to hire Chan as a part-time teacher for a salary of USD$60 a month. It wasn't much; however, it was more than he was getting at the commune office, and he could trust that we would actually pay him on time each month. Chan was grateful, and our paid team had become four.

Now that we had a permanent team, Human and Hope Association had the personnel to work on new projects. The first new project I was keen to start was one that promoted creativity amongst our students. I had learnt from my team that repetitive learning was prevalent in public schools, and students weren't encouraged to think outside the box. I went about researching a few weeks of lesson plans and put a call out to my Facebook network for funding. Within a few days, one friend in Australia held a small fundraiser and donated enough funds for us to launch this new project. I headed out to the local stationery shop, and with my wallet containing one hundred dollars in cash, I purchased the paint, paper, scissors, glue, and glitter that we needed to run the lessons.

We decided to cap the number of students who would attend our art class at 40. As we had six local volunteers and staff members who would teach the class, this enabled us to provide the students with more personalised assistance. To recruit students, we put an announcement and sign-up sheet on the announcement board at Human and Hope Association a week before class was due to start. Within three days, the list was full, and we were ready to go!

Of course, the first Sunday of art class was organised chaos. In typical Khmer style, instead of just the 40 registered students turning up, we had 83 students in total. We began the lesson with a balloon relay race game, and with students consistently turning up late during the game, the fun lasted longer than I had planned. Then came the art activity. I wanted to start this project with simple artwork, so the students could gain their confidence with trying new ways of doing things and encourage them to come up with their own ideas. With plenty of coloured paper, they cut out shapes to create sceneries on A4 pieces of paper. There were choruses of 'I don't have the ability to do this' and 'I don't know what to do', however, with the encouragement of our team, at the end of the lesson, we had 83 gorgeous pieces of artwork, which we hung up along pieces of string on the downstairs balcony.

The plan was to finish the lesson with a movie on our new flat-screen TV, but with an all-day blackout, that didn't happen. Due to the sheer number of students, we decided to divide them into two groups, so one group would attend in the first and third week of every month, and the other group would attend in the second and fourth week. This never happened.

After the initial excitement of the first week of art class, the attendance dropped significantly, with around 30 students attending each Sunday, though that was never constant. We learnt that many of them were required to stay at home to clean and cook, or walk their livestock, or look after their siblings. Since Sunday was the only day they weren't at public school, additional education, particularly that in which their parents didn't understand the merit, took a back seat.

I didn't let this disappoint me or stop my passion. I could see the positive changes in our students who frequently attended art class. Their 'I can't' turned into 'I can', which turned into 'I did it'. Over the next few months, I demonstrated to two of our education team members how to research art activities, the magic that is Pinterest, and how to plan lessons. Their creativity emerged, and by October 2013, I had handed the responsibilities of art class entirely over to them. It worked better that way; instead of purchasing new art supplies, they began utilising recycled materials that reduced our costs and made the activities more accessible for the students to complete at home. This was the first of many examples of the local way being the best way.

IN JANUARY 2013, I was introduced to a friend of a friend who came to visit Human and Hope Association. When I mentioned our dream of having a preschool class for the four-year-olds and five-year-olds in our community, her family immediately jumped on board as monthly donors to help us achieve this.

The reasoning behind starting the preschool program was that many children in the community were unable to be cared for by their parents who had to work hard all day, every day, just to put food on the table. These young children either had to go to work with their parents, stay at home unsupervised, or work themselves collecting vegetables from the forest or picking up rubbish from the street to resell. If these children were in the preschool program for two hours a day, we would hopefully encourage them to see the importance and value of education and it would make the transition to public school easier.

It took two months to plan the program and recruit the students. Heng and Chan got their first taste of community outreach when they were given the tedious task to identify community members who were classified as 'poverty level one and two' (meaning they lived below the national poverty line) and encourage them to send their children to preschool. Some parents were thrilled with the idea of accessing free education for their children. Others were hesitant, as they didn't have anyone who could bring their children to school each day and drop them home. As we were still familiarising ourselves with the community and vice versa, we had to work hard to build up their trust. In the end, Heng and Chan managed to recruit 10 students from our community, all ranging in age from three to five years.

With help from an Australian preschool teacher in Phnom Penh, I developed a structured one-month curriculum that included teaching the students the Khmer alphabet, playtime, movies, art, story time and good habits. Two weeks later, we realised this wasn't going to work. The students had never been in a classroom before, and they were not used to structure, or listening to teachers. At first, Heng and Chan doubted their ability to run the class; after discussing how to move forward, they began working on a flexible daily schedule.

A typical day involved the students arriving by 8am, and starting the day off with a roll call, where they stood in line and followed instructions by the teacher, as is performed at public school in Cambodia. They then headed to the water pump at the back of the building and washed their hands and brushed their teeth. Before attending preschool, *none* of the students had brushed their teeth before, so there were some tears involved for the first few weeks.

It was then time to learn Khmer, a language that has 33 consonants, 16 dependent vowels, and 13 independent vowels. It was no easy feat, nonetheless, most students picked up reading and writing the alphabet and numbers within the first year and were ahead of their classmates at public school once they made the transition.

After studying Khmer, the students then had free play time. I had travelled to Phnom Penh and purchased a range of educational toys for preschool class, most of which were broken within the first few weeks. This didn't deter the students, and they continued to take joy in playing with torn, stuffed animals, limbless dolls, and cars with missing wheels for years to come. Free playtime would be followed by an additional Khmer language lesson, then wrapped up with a 15-minute stint of an educational television show. On Fridays, they learnt about good habits such as road safety, taking care with electricity, and how to be a good student. When the class finished at 10am each day their older siblings, parents or grandparents would arrive and take them home, though sometimes they would be forgotten as life got in the way.

The transformation in the students was incredible. The teachers would proudly talk about the day when the students learnt to use chalk for the first time with their individual chalkboards, when they learnt to sing a song in Khmer, and when the youngest student, at three years old, managed to follow instructions after two months of trying. Despite their hesitations at first, the teachers began to be proactive in thinking of ways to improve the program, and they developed a real passion for each individual student.

Between March and October, two students dropped out. One, who was the most challenging student as he was used to getting whatever he wanted, moved with his family to another rural village. The second student was a three-year-old. The teachers hadn't realised just how young this child was when they recruited her, and she struggled to survive in a class surrounded by children more developed than her. She would cry every day when she was brought to class, and her parents eventually decided that it wasn't the right time for her.

In October 2013, one of our preschool students who had turned six was able to make the transition to public school. Heng went to the local school that was conveniently situated next to Human and Hope Association and enrolled the student in class after consulting with his parents. I made graduation hats, and we had our art class students make decorations, so we could hold a ceremony. We invited the parents of all our students, so they could see the progress that had been made and presented the graduating student with a backpack and study supplies. The class recited the alphabet and sung songs, and the parents laughed and applauded. We beamed with pride, knowing that we were onto a good thing.

The student who graduated in 2013 ended up being the only student in all our years of the preschool class to drop out of public school. Unfortunately, he struggled in the classroom environment, and as his parents had never been afforded the opportunity to study themselves, they didn't persevere in encouraging him to attend. Despite our attempts to keep him there, there was only so much our staff could do.

ON THE DAY WE launched the preschool class, the director came to me with some surprising news. He was going to leave the monkhood.

At first, I was excited. This meant that he could commit more time to Human and Hope Association, and I could work more closely with him without being afraid that my feet would accidentally touch his under the table (a no-no in the monkhood).

A week before his ceremony to release him from the monkhood, tragedy struck. Some of the pagoda committee members and monks had travelled to a religious ceremony a couple of hundred kilometres from Siem Reap. On their way back, one of the cars was involved in an accident that killed a committee member.

The director came to me out of breath whilst I was in art class, panic in his voice, telling me he had to go. I saw him rush over to the monk's lunch area, as more and more villagers gathered in hushed silence. I soon learnt that the head monk had suffered minor injuries, another monk had suffered serious back injuries, and the third monk had suffered head injuries that left him unconscious and in critical condition. He was sent to a private hospital in Siem

IT'S NOT ABOUT ME

Reap that refused to help him as they believed he was at death's door and didn't want that on their conscience. The monk was then transported to a hospital in Phnom Penh, where for two days we waited for news of his condition.

The doctors informed the monk's parents that he wasn't going to survive. Cambodians believe that bad luck will be brought upon the deceased in their next life if they die away from their homeland, so the family scraped together the funds to transport the monk back to Siem Reap so he could pass in peace. Tragically, he died on the journey home.

The director and our team were devastated. This monk was only around 20 years old, and he was a kind soul who had helped make our classroom desks for us. Three of his siblings studied at Human and Hope Association, and we knew that his family was living in poverty. As funerals can be quite expensive, I felt I had to do something. I put a call out to my networks, and in two short days, was able to raise USD$1,000 to donate to the family to help reduce their financial burden.

We cancelled our evening classes the day before the funeral, and all our students went about cleaning the area where the cremation would take place. The next evening, over one hundred of our students attended the funeral with hundreds of additional villagers. I took photos for the family, who had all shaved their heads to represent the end of ties between their deceased son and brother. It was a sad ceremony, with the reality cemented when a bow and arrow lit with fire was shot into the coffin for the cremation.

The next day, the grieving director quietly left monkhood. As a result, the next few months were turbulent, with an array of challenges ahead.

SOMETHING I QUICKLY CAME to realise was the great variation in teaching ability and commitment amongst the volunteers. Although we had begun workshops aimed at enhancing teaching skills, they wouldn't always turn up, or when they did, they would talk through them. I would sometimes walk around observing the classes in the evenings, and I noticed that some teachers were failing to capture the attention of their students or were struggling to engage with the class. Some teachers also failed to turn up to class at all or were consistently late.

Although this had started as a volunteer-run organisation, we were progressing, and to achieve what we wanted, we needed committed, qualified teachers. We were giving them the opportunities: weekly workshops, one-on-one feedback, and more structured curriculums. But if they didn't want to move forward with us, we couldn't let them hold us back.

The first time we told a volunteer she was no longer required was very difficult. For weeks, I had noticed that this volunteer, *Davy, didn't take any notice of the feedback to improve her teaching. She struggled to control her class, given she had permitted 40 students

IT'S NOT ABOUT ME

to join, and as a result, half of the students failed their end-of-term exams.

I approached the director and expressed my concerns. He didn't see Davy's performance as an issue, so I told him with determination that we should let her go. Davy was a volunteer (with a stipend of USD$0.50 per lesson), so there were no regulations in the Cambodian labour law we had to abide by. We were free to let her go and recruit a new volunteer. Of course, the director wouldn't hear me. I pleaded my case, speaking about the importance of quality education for our students, who needed to be learning English the correct way, or they would end up with a sub-standard dialect. He said that we couldn't possibly let her go; she was one of the founding members of Human and Hope Association, and a friend to everyone there. If we let Davy go, she would lose face. I continued to plead my case, my unfortunate temper flaring. Heated arguments aren't the way to achieve anything in Cambodia, as Khmer people tend to switch off and ignore you. Which is exactly what the director did, with Heng, Chan, and Thai (one of our volunteer teachers) watching on.

I left Human and Hope Association that day fuming. How were we supposed to help our students break the cycle of poverty if the English lessons they were being taught weren't getting through to them? Why wouldn't the director put the wellbeing of our community over one person 'losing face'?

When I arrived home, I logged onto the internet and started venting to our main donor at the time. She agreed with me that Davy had to go for the wellbeing of Human and Hope Association, and that she wouldn't pay for Davy's stipend anymore. That was the first in a long line of mistakes I made; I shouldn't have gotten this donor so involved with Human and Hope Association's operations. For the team to have an empowering environment, we needed to ensure donors weren't going to pull the strings. The same went for me.

That evening, after having eaten a family-sized deep-pan pizza, garlic bread, and a bottle of Coke, I was lying in bed regretting my emotional eating when I received a phone call from the director. He told me that he, Heng, Chan and Thai were on their way over to my house. At nine in the evening.

I quickly headed outside and waited waited on my balcony for them to arrive. A few minutes later, that they did, and as they nervously walked up the stairs to my balcony, I greeted them somberly. One of my personal downfalls has always been holding a grudge, and that is what I was doing then. As I led the guys to the pillows on my balcony, it became obvious they had come over for damage control. Over the next 45 minutes, we all spoke our opinion on the situation with Davy. I was adamant that she needed to go, yet they kept saying she should stay, with nothing solid to back up their opinion. It was only when I pulled out my trump card that funding for her role would stop, that they took me seriously. I sadly used my white privilege to get what I wanted, justifying to myself that it was in the best interests of Human and Hope Association.

I wasn't perfect; although I was committed to providing an empowering environment for the team, I let my feelings get the better of me and was forcing my opinion on the very people I was supposed to be helping. My strategy worked, and the team reluctantly agreed that the director would let Davy go, and that we would find someone to replace her. Even though I had gotten the outcome I wanted, I wasn't happy. It made me feel guilty that we had to argue to agree on the action that I had thought should have been accepted in the first place. I didn't want to be the foreigner who came in and told the local staff what to do; I wanted to be the person providing them with the opportunities to make these tough decisions themselves. Throughout my time at Human and Hope Association, I faced more of these challenging situations that always made me question whether or not I had the patience, the cultural knowledge and the resilience for my role.

When the director met with Davy the next day, it was possibly the first time he had to have such a difficult conversation. I saw her leave Human and Hope Association in tears and afterwards, I was approached by two other volunteers who disagreed with our decision. To this day, I don't regret letting Davy go; what I do regret is the way I handled the situation. Reflecting on it has helped me grow and understand more about our value of empowerment, which was a critical change when we had to let a staff member go in 2016. Davy leaving meant we were finally moving forward with the quality of our volunteers and showing the others that we expected the best from them, so we could provide our community with the best education.

WE NEEDED TO FIND a volunteer to replace Davy, and it just so happened that Thai's brother, Sokrithy*, had recently left the monkhood. Whilst living at the pagoda, he had set up an English school for the children in his community, 60km from Siem Reap, so I was interested to see if he wanted to volunteer with us. Knowing where he lived, I drove by Sokrithy's house one day to converse with him in English. Satisfied with his level of fluency, I asked if he wanted to teach for two hours an evening once he finished his construction work. He agreed and began the next week when our new term commenced.

With the new term beginning, we were able to cut the class sizes down. Working with the team, I tried to get them to understand that we needed to focus on quality instead of quantity. There was no point in educating 30 children in a class if the teachers couldn't give them the attention they needed. To begin with, we capped the class sizes at 20, and this was later reduced to 18.

It didn't take long for the volunteers to get used to this way of thinking. They had been brought up in a public-school system where there were upwards of seventy students in a class. Although the class sizes at Human and Hope Association were much smaller than what they were familiar with, they found it easier to capture the students' attention and found that their English levels improved quicker.

One day in March 2013, the director came to me with a pleasant surprise. Our NGO registration certificates had arrived, and we were officially a non-government organisation in Cambodia! I breathed a sigh of relief, then proceeded to do a happy dance.

I then went about planning a party to celebrate our registration. With the help of our students, we prepared decorations and photo boards to spice up the party. We organised for Chan's mother to prepare a Khmer barbeque, and ordered three cakes with the individual letters 'HHA' for our guests to indulge in. We invited our community partners, staff, their parents, and key villagers to help us commemorate the fact that we were able to register our NGO in just five months. It was just what we needed to put the issue with Davy behind us. Or so I thought.

8. Crime and Safety

IN GENERAL, SIEM REAP is a safe place to visit. However, like any city, you should always be alert and aware of your surroundings. There are numerous scams that go on in town, and around the popular holidays more thieves tend to emerge.

My first brush with danger was in March 2012. I had been living in a studio apartment that was part of a building with a total of eight rooms. The Khmer landlords lived in a separate, run-down wooden house next to my room. It was a very simple apartment; when you walked through the door, I had an orange wicker couch to the right, a double bed to the left, and straight ahead was a small kitchen with another door leading out to the back of the compound. To the left of the kitchen was a bathroom that only disbursed cold water.

Although it wasn't ideal, this apartment cost me USD$60 a month to rent, plus water and electricity. I lived on a very tight budget the whole time I was in Cambodia, and this was all I could afford. Every night, the gate at the compound was locked, though it was easy enough for someone to climb over the fence. For my peace of mind, I used to move my couch against my front door every night, though if someone did want to break in, it was very easy to pick the lock and push my bamboo couch away.

One day during working hours, I stopped off at my apartment as I needed to grab some money to buy things for the school I was originally working for. I had been lending them money as they hadn't been able to get to the bank due to the director being off work. Once I took my cash, there was USD$100 left in my wallet, which should have lasted me for three weeks, yet the next day when I went back to my wallet, that $100 note was gone. I was shocked and looked everywhere to see if it had fallen out, but that precious bill was nowhere to be found. Later that evening while dining out with a friend, she suggested that I may have been mistaken when remembering how much cash I had, so I let it go.

A few days later, after having been reimbursed USD$150 for other costs, I went to my wallet to grab some cash. When I opened my wallet, I realised all my money was gone. I had not been mistaken – someone *had* stolen from me. Twice. They had not taken anything else in my apartment; they had known exactly what to grab and where to grab it from, and had stolen USD$250 in total, which was the amount of money I had expected to live off for a month.

My heart started beating rapidly, and in a state of shock, I phoned my friend, a Peace Corps volunteer who worked with me at the organisation. He was with his friend and told me he would be over in 20 minutes.

He was over in five. After coming in and discussing the situation, we decided it was best I got out of the apartment straight away. With the help of his friend, we went to the landlord who told us that despite being at home all day, every day, she hadn't seen any suspicious activity. Given I had previously witnessed her opening my apartment door by sliding a card between the door and the wall, I had my suspicions.

My friend's brother called a tuk-tuk and we started quickly taking all my photos and artworks off the wall. We then grabbed all my possessions and shoved them into big plastic bags I still had from my move at the start of the year. The decision was to leave my furniture and kitchen appliances at the apartment, but to take everything else over to my friend's office where she also lived. At the time, she had a spare bedroom and allowed me to stay there until I found a place. Sitting on the armrest, hanging out of the tuk-tuk, we drove with all my worldly possessions to my friend's office, my friend following behind on my bicycle.

Thanks to the support of my friends, I was able to move on from that incident, though the feeling never left me that someone had been through my personal space and belongings

PHNOM PENH IS THE capital of Cambodia, and I don't like it one bit. It is notorious for its petty street crime, and although many foreigners love it and call it home, I tend to avoid it like the plague. In 2014, when my friend Andrea came to visit, we ventured to Phnom Penh. She treated us to a luxurious hotel room, and we spent our days shopping for fabric for Human and Hope Association's sewing business and sightseeing. We were driven around in a purple tuk-tuk that had mesh on the sides to prevent bag snatchers, though this wasn't much help. I was looking at photos I had taken on my iPad mini when I saw something out of the corner of my eye. Living in Cambodia, I had taught myself to always be alert so I could avoid potential danger. This came in handy that day, as I looked up just in time to see two men on a motorbike driving beside our tuk-tuk, with one reaching over to grab my iPad. I clutched my iPad whilst moving my body to the right and kicked at the man with my left leg whilst his fingers came dangerously close to my iPad. He had a smile on his face the whole time. Knowing they wouldn't be successful in this instance, they then sped off. We stopped up the road and our tuk-tuk driver told the police that were standing on a street corner what had happened. The incident left me feeling violated, just like I felt when my apartment was robbed. It had an extra level of emotion to it though, as I had been able to look the perpetrators in the eye. I was extremely cautious for that trip, and never took anything out of my bag for a trip in a Phnom Penh tuk-tuk again.

In 2016, I stayed in Phnom Penh for three nights, as my new job required me to attend some meetings in the big smoke. One morning I was feeling poorly, so I missed the morning meetings. My boss picked me up in a tuk-tuk after lunch, and we headed to our afternoon meeting. Before doing that, however, the staff at my hotel reminded me to hold onto my backpack as there were many bag snatchers about. I jumped into the tuk-tuk and we set off to our meeting. With my backpack strapped around my front and a lock on the zippers, I still didn't feel secure, but it was the best I could do. As we approached our destination, our tuk-tuk driver paused at the top of a small hill. My boss leaned over to talk to the driver and guide him, when at that moment, a man on a motorbike who was also at the top of this small hill suddenly turned his motorbike around, came straight for our tuk-tuk, reached in and grabbed my bosses backpack that had been sitting on the floor, and took off with it. It all happened in a matter of seconds. My boss jumped out of the tuk-tuk and ran after the thief, though it was no use. The thief was long gone, with a MacBook, cash, and credit cards. My boss, being the true professional he is, ensured we still attended our scheduled meeting and stayed calm and in control. Afterwards, we went to the local police station and spoke to a policeman who couldn't care less about the robbery. It was clear we weren't going to be getting his possessions back.

Our tuk-tuk driver was very apologetic and kept assuring us that he had worked for the UN as a car driver for several years. He was to be trusted, he explained to us. He hadn't called a friend with the location of our tuk-tuk, as some drivers had been known to do. We knew he wasn't to blame, yet the next day when he took me to the airport, he brought along certificates of recommendation from the UN to prove his innocence. That was thankfully the last time I visited Phnom Penh, and I have no intention to return soon.

ALTHOUGH SIEM REAP IS a lot different to Phnom Penh, you generally still need to exercise caution. After a few months of living there, I realised that I shouldn't be riding around by myself at night time. When I went out with my colleagues, they would always ensure that someone accompanied me home, and that there was someone to accompany the person who accompanied me home. The road I used to live near was known for robberies and bag snatchings. One of my friends was once robbed on the street where I lived and pulled off her bicycle, causing head injuries. Another friend of mine was once held down by street children and slapped repeatedly when she wouldn't give them money. And another friend was punched in the face when she ran after a child who had stolen her friend's phone while they were waiting in line at a bar.

Aside from the violence intentionally caused by perpetrators, there was also plenty of unintentional injuries and deaths caused by negligence. In November 2014, five people were killed when a fire ripped through a nightclub in Siem Reap.[xi] Their charred bodies were displayed on the grounds of a nearby pagoda, signifying they were unable to escape from the windowless club. My students told me that there were many more people who perished in the fire, and that their bodies had been removed by a garbage truck. One of my students was adamant that his friend had been bartending, and after that night she had never been seen again, despite not being on the list of deceased. She had left behind a young daughter. I used to visit that club when I first lived in Siem Reap, however, the enclosed spaces left me hyperventilating, plus the cover charge was USD$3, an exorbitant amount for Cambodians, so I didn't return.

A month after I first moved to Siem Reap, a fire ripped through some houses and shops along the river. It seemed that everyone was connected to a family affected by it. The owner of my guesthouse told me her cousin had lost everything, and the aunt and uncle of my colleague had almost lost their house. My colleague told me that the firefighters had turned up, yet just stood there watching and didn't take any action. These families who lived and had businesses along the river were due to be relocated to Sambour Commune, where Human and Hope Association was later located, as Siem Reap River was going to be expanded. Rumours circulated around town that the fire had been deliberately lit to 'encourage' the remaining villagers to move, though of course these rumours were dismissed by local officials. Altogether,

27 shops that were also used as houses were destroyed.[xii]

Fire is often caused by electrical faults. If you have ever been to Cambodia or Southeast Asia, you will understand why. There are usually dozens of electrical wires that are tangled between each other on the top of electrical poles; many electricians are not formally trained, and the source of electricity is unstable. One day in 2012, I came home to my wooden house and smelt smoke. I wasn't sure where it was coming from, so I went around my house sniffing about until I came to the source. My fridge was on fire! At that moment, my housemate came home, and unsure what to do, we ran down the stairs while I called out to my landlord, 'Help us, help us, help us!' (which, fun fact, I realised I was pronouncing incorrectly and yelling, 'F**k us, f**k us, f**k us!'). She bolted up the stairs, turned off the electricity at the source and put out the fire. My housemate and I stood there in shock. Had we not come home when we did, our second storey, wooden, Khmer house would have been engulfed by flames. Not only that, had our landlord not been home, we wouldn't have known what to do, as I had never come across an electrical fire before. From that day on, I was extra cautious when using electrical sockets.

WHEN WE WERE HOLDING a regular management meeting one day in early 2015, I asked my colleague how his weekend was.

'My nephew was hit by a car and he died,' he told me.

'Oh, my gosh, I am so sorry to hear that. That is terrible,' I replied. 'What happened?'

'He was playing near his house and the neighbour reversed the car and hit him.'

'How old was he?' I asked

'One,' he responded, sadness in his eyes.

'Please, go home,' I told him. 'You can take as much time off as you want.'

'No, it's okay,' he replied. 'We already had the funeral for him, and since he was so young, we don't do much for him.'

Despite trying to persuade him that he should take time off, my colleague was adamant that he wanted to be at work. His nephew was never mentioned again.

THE DANGEROUS ROADS ALSO left me fearing for my safety in Cambodia. I had plenty of near misses when riding on my motorbike, and others due to the condition of the roads combined with a general lack of road safety knowledge by many citizens.

One day in 2015, a large hole appeared in the road leading to Human and Hope Association. I don't know how it got to be that size. Did a big truck go over the road at the wrong time and create the hole? Did it collapse one evening due to poor quality? Even now I am unsure how it happened. One day the hole wasn't there, the next day it was. For a few days, I drove

IT'S NOT ABOUT ME

around the hole on the way to work, not really bothered with the fact that it could be quite easy to fall into it given that it took up half the road and was easily three-metres deep.

Then one day, the repairs started. However, the repairs started in the rainy season, so when they made the hole larger to start their work on it, the big hole filled up with water. Boy, did that put the repairs back! The hole eventually took up the width of the road, and the only way around it was by taking a sharp turn and driving through a sawmill. The problem with doing that was that it was such a busy detour, and people didn't honk on the way around the sharp corner; accidents were bound to happen. So, I started taking a long way to work, increasing my travel time by 10 minutes.

Almost six months later, the hole was finally fixed. I could finally get to work under half an hour. However, during the time that the hole was being fixed, about 100m further down the road, a new hole was being created. Well, not a hole exactly, but the side of the road was breaking off and only about three quarters of the road was useable. So, two days after the other hole was finally fixed, work started on the new hole. This time, they also made the hole into the width of the road and impossible to get around.

On the first day, I followed villagers on their motorbikes through a field to get around it. That route turned out to be quite dangerous, so I turned back and found another route. I ended up taking that route over the next few weeks, as it took quite some time to repair that hole. Whether the builders take a short or long amount of time, the road usually breaks again within weeks or months. This is often due to low quality supplies, taking shortcuts or skimming off allocated funds.

I would often find myself riding through potholes, almost falling off my motorbike. Or, if it was the rainy season, I would end up in flood water before realising the depth of the situation, and ride through dirty water that reached the top of my tires. A few of my colleagues had accidents during the time I was at Human and Hope Association, however, thanks to our strict helmet policy, they only had minor injuries. One time when Heng and I went into town to buy supplies for preschool, we ended up with too many items to drive home with. We called Thai, who took Heng back to the office with some supplies while we tied the rest to my motorbike. As I followed them on my motorbike, another driver cut in front of me, so I wasn't directly behind my colleagues anymore. Just as that was happening, a man came driving down the narrow and busy road towards us. He was going faster than anyone else on the road, and with a cart attached to the back of his motorbike, it was an accident waiting to happen. Which it did, about five seconds later. The woman on the motorbike in front of him suddenly stopped at a shop and given that indicators are rarely used in Cambodia, the speeding driver behind them wasn't prepared. He tried to brake too late, but given how fast he had been driving, this wasn't going to work. His cart veered off to the left while his motorbike (and him) fell, smashing into the man who had overtaken me, causing him to fall off his motorbike and onto the road. Debris hit Human and Hope Association's motorbike and chipped off some of the frame, whilst I managed to brake just in time, so I didn't run over the man in front of me. It all happened in a matter of seconds, and pure luck had meant that I wasn't the one who bore the brunt of the impact. Fortunately, the men didn't appear to be seriously injured, so we continued our journey back to Human and Hope Association, knowing we just had a very close call.

SALLY HETHERINGTON OAM

9. The Pitfalls of Voluntourism and Poverty Tourism

AS MANY AS 10 million people a year are cumulatively spending up to $2 billion a year on voluntourism activities.[xiii] Voluntourism is short-term or one-off volunteering overseas, and it has many benefits. People often say it gives them a sense of meaning, and they feel wanted and appreciated. For others, it meets their need of wanting to volunteer *and* travel. It can also help you develop your experience, and it looks great on your C.V. You can gain insight into the developing world, and who can forget how good it makes you feel?

Did you notice a pattern about those points? The benefits were all about the voluntourist. There is no consideration given to the impact on the beneficiary, which can often be negative. But how could helping possibly have a negative impact?

'It is important for NGOs to be run by Cambodians. By doing so, we can help young generations show their ability to lead NGOs.'
– Ngoy Bunrong, Human and Hope Association

WE ENDED THE FOREIGN volunteer program at Human and Hope Association in two parts. The first step was to stop using foreign English teaching volunteers. The second phase was to only accept volunteers that could work directly with the staff, providing them with training that we couldn't yet afford to pay for. From it, they learnt first aid, human resources, techniques for teaching English effectively, skills to work with young children, and product development.

Our last foreign volunteer came to Human and Hope Association in 2014, and after that we ended the program. Although we had gotten excellent value out of the volunteers who were there to train the staff, our team had enough knowledge and a great succession plan, so we didn't require assistance any more. By this time, we had secured funding for our team to participate in external workshops run by experienced local training companies, a few of our team members were studying in university or English school on scholarships, and I was still holding weekly development workshops, which were eventually entirely taken over by our local staff and Khmer board and volunteers. Together, our team wrote down the reasons why we would no longer be accepting foreign volunteers.

Empowerment of staff – Our mission is to empower Cambodians to create sustainable futures for themselves. We believe in applying this mission not just to our beneficiaries, but to our staff as well. Therefore, it is important to give our staff the opportunity to thrive in their roles and gain confidence. We have seen first-hand that when volunteers come into organisations, the effects can often be disempowering, as the local staff believe that they cannot fulfil their jobs without the support of foreigners. We consider local people to be the subject matter experts, as they are the ones who know the country and traditions best. By promoting team work amongst the local staff and community, they can learn from each other and not become reliant on foreigners.

Consistency – When volunteers come and go, it creates an inconsistency with our education system which follows lesson plans and a curriculum that is developed well in advance. In the past, students complained of volunteers who didn't teach them effectively. Furthermore, we educate many students who come from disadvantaged and vulnerable backgrounds, and having strangers come and go in their lives creates an unstable situation on top of what they already experience at their homes. By having full-time staff to teach our students and provide support to the community, we can create a trustworthy relationship with our beneficiaries.

Child protection – Child abuse is prevalent in Cambodia, and our staff and visitors must adhere to a strict child protection policy. By inviting large numbers of temporary volunteers, the risk of abuse is heightened. Our local staff have been trained in child protection and are equipped to deal with this issue in a local context.

Culture – The Khmer culture is unique, and there are often complex factors contributing to situations. Often volunteers who come for a short period of time inadvertently offend the local staff and students by not adhering to the culture. Our local staff can effectively work with the community in a culturally sensitive way and therefore gain the best outcomes.

Attachment issues – In the past, the staff have formed good relationships with some volunteers. When volunteers left, the staff ended up feeling quite down, and this affected their work. There have been situations where our students also experience these feelings which goes against our aim of creating a stable environment, as they already have challenging lives.

Language barriers – The official language of Cambodia is Khmer, which all our staff speak. However, as our projects aren't just focused on English class, we have several staff who speak minimal or no English, and communication can be very difficult. This often proves to be frustrating for both our staff and volunteers and can result in strained relationships for all parties involved.

Sustainability – Having volunteers come and go isn't sustainable. What *is* sustainable is training local staff, who can in turn, train more local staff as part of a succession plan. That way if a key staff member leaves, we have someone else to take their place, and business can continue as usual.

Time – To run an effective volunteer program takes a lot of time, with the pre-arrival, volunteer duration and post-departure. In the past, we have found it very time consuming to look after volunteers, with staff members commenting they have spent more time concentrating on the volunteers than our beneficiaries. This takes time away from our crucial work with the local community and in building the capacity of the local staff.

'Khmer people understand the needs of their community the best. When we run our own NGOs, we encourage Cambodians to work independently. It is also much easier for us to work with and cooperate with the government. When NGOs accept foreign volunteers, it can sometimes be difficult to work with them because of different cultures. It also takes a lot of our time to arrange work for them.'
– Doeung Savdy, Human and Hope Association

A COUPLE OF YEARS ago, I was shocked to come across a new voluntourism cruise. This was the first cruise line dedicated entirely to voluntourism, offering seven-day volunteer cruises. That's right, *seven days* to make an impact in a low-income country. The ship carries 700 passengers and sails year-round to the Dominican Republic.

There were several different voluntourism activities on offer. I call them activities, as that is exactly what they are.

Environmental – People could participate in the production and distribution of more than 5,000 clay water filters. But wouldn't it have been better to donate money so that local workers could earn a salary to make these filters instead?

Education – Cruise participants were given the opportunity to work with students and other community members to help them improve their English skills. Instead of moving in and out of these children's lives, wouldn't it be more beneficial to support the stipend for a long-term volunteer who could build capacity for local teachers, there so that the students could engage in English conversation with their teachers instead?

Economic development – Travellers were told they could have a 'positive, hands-on impact' in the cultivation of cacao plants and recycled paper crafts. How about instead of doing that, tourists shopped at the craft shop and supported the local economy?

It seemed to me that this cruise was just to make people feel good about themselves, not to have a positive and lasting impact on the community. This is a trap that people fall into when wanting to volunteer overseas; they participate in tasks that give them a sense of engagement with the local community, not realising they can be disrupting the whole society. I don't blame voluntourists; it is the companies and

NGOs that need to be rethinking their strategies and putting the community first instead of profit. When their focus is on the voluntourists' experience, it is likely that there will be harmful interactions between the locals and voluntourists. By changing the system, we can change the way people think, and instead encourage them to interact with community members in more respectful, empowering and sustainable ways, such as by supporting social enterprises and local businesses.

Conducting outreach in the community.

THERE ARE NUMEROUS ORGANISATIONS in Cambodia that encourage people to visit for a week and build a house. I, for one, would *never* think of doing this, as I am not qualified. I wouldn't be able to build a house in Australia without experience or qualifications, so why would I go to Cambodia or any other country to do so?

IT'S NOT ABOUT ME

If you have been reading this chapter thinking, *Sally is right, I shouldn't head overseas to teach voluntarily, well done!* I am glad I have reached somebody. But if you are also thinking, *However, I could do something other than teach, there are many needy people around*, I am here to implore you otherwise.

In Pippa Biddle's essay, *The Problem with Little White Girls (and Boys): Why I Stopped Being a Voluntourist* xxxiv she reflects on her building trip to Tanzania.

'In high school, I travelled to Tanzania as part of a school trip. There were 14 white girls, 1 black girl who, to her frustration, was called white by almost everyone we met in Tanzania, and a few teachers/chaperones. $3,000 bought us a week at an orphanage, a half-built library, and a few pickup soccer games, followed by a week-long safari.

Our mission while at the orphanage was to build a library. Turns out that we, a group of highly educated, private boarding school students were so bad at the most basic construction work that each night the men had to take down the structurally unsound bricks we had laid and rebuild the structure so that, when we woke up in the morning, we would be unaware of our failure. It is likely that this was a daily ritual. Us mixing cement and laying bricks for 6+ hours, them undoing our work after the sunset, re-laying the bricks, and then acting as if nothing had happened so that the cycle could continue.

Basically, we failed at the sole purpose of our being there. It would have been more cost-effective, stimulative of the local economy, and efficient for the orphanage to take our money and hire locals to do the work, but there we were trying to build straight walls without a level.'

If you were interested in building a house as part of a voluntourism trip, ask yourself the following questions first.

Am I qualified? Are you a builder in your country? Do you have the skills and knowledge to build a house? If you aren't qualified, there are issues with both your safety and the safety of the family that will be living in the house.

Could a local do that job? Hiring local workers to do a job is much more sustainable. There are currently over 600,000 Cambodians (almost 4% of the population)[xiv] living and working in Thailand, as they are unable to secure employment in-country. If they take the journey by foot, they are at risk of stepping on one of the hundreds of thousands of landmines that are still scattered around the country after civil war. Once they successfully reach the Thai/Cambodia border, there is a chance they will be shot by police. Once they reach Thailand and gain employment, they risk unfair working conditions and exploitation from their employers. Furthermore, if they illegally enter Thailand, the chance of them getting arrested for unlawful entry is high. By supporting local workers to build that house, you are contributing to whole families and communities, and making a much bigger impact than if you were to build that house yourself.

Who will take care of maintenance? Building a house, water well, school, toilet or play equipment doesn't just end there. Ongoing maintenance is needed. One of our sewing students at Human and Hope Association had a water well built a few years back. Once it stopped working, they didn't have the money to pay for the maintenance, nor was any ongoing support offered. The well sat unused for a long time, with the student and her family relying on the generosity of their neighbours to let them use their well. If you are participating in voluntourism with a company, how are they ensuring that maintenance is taken care of? Do they follow-up with the families? Do they have a support liaison?

Is this a long-term solution? Whether you are building a house or donating one, is it a long-term solution? Will this bring a family out of poverty? Will this create a dependence on aid? Will this cause them to stop seeking employment opportunities? There are so many questions to ask yourself.

As Jacob Kushner said in his 2016 article *The Voluntourist's Dilemma*, easing global poverty is an enormously complex task that requires hard, sustained work, and expertise[xv]. Although we don't want to hear this, we do need to acknowledge that we most likely don't have the expertise to solve poverty and social issues, nor may our direct input actually be needed.

'Foreigners have a very different culture to Cambodians, which can cause issues. When we encourage Cambodians to run NGOs, we can demonstrate a strong communication between NGOs and community members. It also shows a willingness for Cambodian people to help each other and focus on sharing skills.'
– Tenh Sopheak, Human and Hope Association

THERE ARE COUNTLESS FOR-PROFIT companies that offer a wide range of experience for voluntourists, such as social work, animal care, building and agriculture, in addition to the standard teaching assignments. You could spend hours browsing their website for endless possibilities of volunteer projects. I have, and I feel anxious every time I do.

One such company offers high-school volunteers to spend half-days painting murals, installing new floors and renovating care centres and schools. Their afternoons will then be spent running activities such as sporting programs with poor children or visiting the local orphanage to play with toddlers. Whilst I do believe we should be promoting altruism in people from an early age, encouraging voluntourism isn't the way to do it. Why can't the organisations ask the students to fundraise instead in their home countries, and hire local workers to put in a new floor or paint a mural? Why should they be running activities for

Nepalese children, when the organisation would have qualified local staff to do that job instead?

These organisations often suggest that the volunteers can make a 'significant difference' in the lives of others through this work. Answer me this - how does painting a mural or playing games with children make a significant difference in other people's lives? I do agree that it would make a difference in your own, as you would have stories to tell, new profile photos for Facebook, and will receive lots of great compliments. Does the image of a foreigner surrounded by a group of smiling local children sound familiar? Is it really appropriate for a group of high school students who aren't qualified to install a floor or work in childcare to be doing so? Doesn't this cause a risk to the people they are helping, and to themselves, in the form of injury or accusations? What about the children they are supposedly helping, developing unstable emotional attachments due to this never-ending revolving door of voluntourists? Yet, so many companies are encouraging this behaviour.

Another company offers public health volunteer roles that are available to anyone over the age of 16, regardless of whether they have medical experience or not. During their time in Cambodia, participants are responsible for conducting non-invasive medical tests in the community and they will also provide basic health services for children at kindergarten centres and schools.

Does anyone see a problem with this? This voluntourism company and the local NGO are encouraging volunteers without the education, skills or experience to conduct medical tests on people. Would you permit someone like that to conduct medical tests on yourself? Would you trust them? I certainly wouldn't. But, as I have mentioned, Cambodians are not used to saying no, for fear of losing face. And sometimes, they will just take what they can get. So, the 'need' continues, even though the delivery is sub-standard.

'Cambodians should help themselves and their own people whenever they can. By running their own NGOs, they can demonstrate the ability to successfully operate organisations on their own. They then become good role models to other organisations that depend on foreigners and give Cambodians confidence in themselves. When Cambodians run their own NGOs, they eliminate the assumption of some Cambodians and foreigners who say that some jobs can only be undertaken by foreign nationals.'
– Phat Phyrom, Human and Hope Association

WHILST WRITING THIS BOOK I hopped on Instagram and searched 'voluntourism', just to let my blood boil. I came across a photo of a white girl surrounded by Cambodian children, so I clicked on the photo to investigate it further. The photo was

IT'S NOT ABOUT ME

taken at an English school that is a short distance from Human and Hope Association. This English school was around before Human and Hope Association moved into Sambour Commune. Our team had decided that our organisations differ enough that it wouldn't matter being close by, as the only thing that we had in common was the English language program. Given the number of school-aged children in our commune that were living in poverty, there still wouldn't be enough opportunities to educate them all, even between the two NGOs.

We took pride in the differences that we could identify between our NGO and the one that was located nearby. The other school was free, their class sizes were not capped, and some community members told us that the teachers didn't appear to have strong classroom management skills. Given that we believe NGOs should share knowledge, we were going to extend an olive branch and invite the staff members from this organisation to our weekly capacity building workshops, so that they could develop their teaching skills.

A few weeks before we moved into our community centre, our opinion changed. My colleague and I had driven past this organisation to visit a sewing student who lived on the same road. I witnessed a dozen or so foreign teenagers at the organisation, playing soccer with the Cambodian students. Then, on the way back, I saw one of those teenagers holding a Cambodian baby and having her friend take photos of her. We realised that if this organisation accepted large groups of foreign visitors and volunteers, their values wouldn't align with ours. We, as an organisation, spoke out against voluntourism and were working towards making myself, the only foreign staff member, redundant. We moved into our community centre in October 2014 and continued offering the same projects we had before: English, Khmer, preschool, art, library, sewing, microfinance, farming, community outreach, and community workshops. I kept an eye on their Facebook page, and noticed an increasing number of foreign volunteers coming in groups to the organisation, planting trees, giving students presents, teaching children, and painting murals.

When I moved back to Australia, the organisation slipped from my mind. When I came across the photo of the voluntourist with students from this organisation on Instagram, I decided to investigate further. And that is when I came across a post from two months prior, stating that their school was going to open a sewing centre that they had already started to build, but required funds for the actual materials to teach with.

This caused me some concern. Sewing isn't like English and not everyone can/wants to be trained in sewing; it takes a big commitment to learn. We had been recruiting sewing students from that commune since July 2013, and it was tough to do so. We had dedicated significant time over the last few years to developing the program so that we could achieve the best outcomes possible for our students, and we finally had a 100% retention rate in the program, with all students earning money from sewing just three months into the course. A nearby church referred students to us, and other NGOs from further away enquired about sending their community members to learn. I wondered why this English school had set up a sewing school when Human and Hope Association already had one and recruited new students every six months from the same community.

Upon further investigation, it appeared that this is exactly what this organisation had done. They built a sewing school without funding for the necessities to run the program. NGO Management 101 – no organisation should set up a project without funding for at least a year. It's not smart, nor is it sustainable. As a result of there being two sewing centres within five hundred metres of each other, there would be an abundance of sewing shops in homes around the area, resulting in less profit for students, and a lower impact on the standard of living.

One solution could have been for the NGO to approach Human and Hope Association for an opportunity to work together, including referring villagers to us, if the NGO saw that there was an increased need for a sewing program.

One of our major issues at Human and Hope Association is finding students to participate in our courses due to a lack of understanding about the importance of taking time out to study, despite having a good name in the community, and constantly promoting our programs. For those villagers who do understand, they gain confidence, are respected role models in their community, and increase their standard of living. Our program has progressed due to a huge commitment on our part, and we want to empower as many villagers as possible.

I notified Human and Hope Association's director and vocational training coordinator about this development, with the director being in the dark as I was. He went straight to the NGO and met with their director. He was informed that although the classroom had been built, they didn't have the funds to run the program yet. The director of the other organisation wouldn't listen to the concerns our director raised about having two sewing centres so close to each other.

My Cambodian partner, also surprised at this development, told me that this is the way that many Cambodian NGOs work. They set up new projects to get money from foreigners, without investigating the need or putting the time and energy needed into the program. It takes an incredible amount of time and effort to recruit students who are living in poverty. He was very concerned that this organisation, lacking the time and experience to do so, would accept anybody into the program, regardless of their existing income. This would then amplify the problem already existing in Siem Reap of people getting things for free when they should be supporting local businesses by paying for training and education if they could afford it.

My concerns were also about the beneficiaries. If the organisation didn't treat every student carefully and address their individual needs, they risked the chance of the student failing in learning their skill and earning a stable income. If the students failed once, history and experience had shown us that the probability of them attempting to study again were low, which resulted in them remaining in poverty and impacting their opinions on educating their children. This could have dire consequences for our community, who had been making fantastic progress in supporting the villagers to break the cycle of poverty for good.

As it turns out, the sewing program never got off the ground, despite the room being built. Although I am unsure what the future holds for this organisation, one thing is for sure. NGOs should be supporting each other and referring possible beneficiaries instead of trying to compete and duplicate niche services.

ANOTHER CONCERNING TREND I came across while in Cambodia was tourists visiting public schools in Cambodia. They interrupt classes, make students pose for photos and pretty much act all high and mighty. In addition to this, many give out presents. By providing children with presents, they are creating a 'normal' image for this kind of behaviour. It shouldn't be normal.

Picture this: Your child/sibling/cousin is sitting in class, learning...I don't know, maybe mathematics.

Concentrating. Trying to work out a formula, trying to make sense of what is before them. They have almost got it. It suddenly starts to dawn on them and... *click, click, click.* A tourist has walked into the classroom. That's right, another one. A stranger who does not know your child/cousin/sibling but is taking photos of them while they are just trying to get an education. The class stops working. They must entertain the tourists, pretend that they matter, just in the hope that the school receives a donation. Smile, laugh, pose for photos, act as though their presence is more important than getting an education. Sooner or later, your child/cousin/sibling will begin to think of this as a normal situation, that foreigners are 'saviours' and that it is just a regular part of their schooling for these outsiders to treat them as tourist attractions.

Would you allow this to happen at your child/cousin/sibling's school? Well, if you lived in Cambodia, it appears you wouldn't have a choice. Many companies offer travel packages that include visits to public schools that are as common as a trip to Angkor Wat. They encourage this kind of behaviour, and independent tour guides and hoteliers are, too.

Being the Facebook stalker I am, (come on, everyone does it), I have come across numerous photos of Human and Hope Association's past and current students on the Facebook pages of tourists and locals. Why? Because they simply were at public school when these people rocked up. Because they wanted an education. Because their parents wanted a better life for them, they were subject to getting photos taken of them and plastered for the world to see.

As smart travellers, we have a choice. We can stand up and say no. We can make informed choices and put ourselves in the shoes of the children and their families. They deserve an uninterrupted education, one that doesn't have conditions on it. If you want to support public school education in Cambodia, *please*, do so! Just do it in a way that doesn't involve photographs and trips to the classroom. I will keep repeating this; we all deserve dignity and respect.

'More Cambodian youth have pursued university education, so it is important to let them use their knowledge and skills to help their own people. When we have the skills to do the job, why do we need volunteers? Yet, so many organisations still accept volunteers for donations. This can cause child protection issues when they are not strict enough in order to satisfy visitors and volunteers by allowing them to play or stay with children and take photos and videos. Unskilled volunteers can also provide a negative impact to the beneficiaries who join the program, which causes problems for a long time. Organisations need to ensure their sustainability, so local staff are crucial as they don't just work for short periods of times like those who partake in voluntourism. When one NGO is run by Cambodians (like Human

and Hope Association), others will learn from it and want to be the same.'

– San Thai, Human and Hope Association

THIS BRINGS ME TO my next point, poverty tourism. This dark form of tourism, also known as slum tourism, dates to the 1800's. Wealthy New Yorkers would travel to the Lower East Side to see how the lower class lived.[xviii] This type of tourism has exploded in recent years, with many tour companies encouraging people to participate in poverty tourism.

I myself used to be a guilty party to poverty tourism. I took photos of children in Myanmar I gave my plastic bottles to in 2008, so they would have something to play with. *Look how happy they are with the simple things in life*, I am sure I captioned the photo as I uploaded it to Facebook for the world to see. It wasn't right then, it isn't right now, and it will never be right.

When we go into the 'slums' or poor villages, we are going into people's homes. We are taking photos of their day-to-day living and intruding in their lives. How would you feel if you were at home, hanging out the washing or taking a bath, and someone came and took photos of you? Violated, perhaps? Not good, I am sure.

I have always felt very strongly about not making our community members around Human and Hope Association targets of 'poverty porn'. Despite constantly needing funding, when a film crew from Singapore asked to film some of our beneficiaries in their dire situations, we said no. This is because every person has the right to privacy, and although some people might agree to having videos and photos taken of them, they most likely don't fully understand what the media will be used for, how they will be portrayed, and the repercussions of this.

A few years ago, there was a huge debate over how an NGO in Cambodia used photos of children in their end of financial year campaign. The goal was to raise funds to provide marginalised children with training opportunities. The organisation used individual photos of children with dirt smeared on their faces and ripped clothing and used captions that referred to the children as sex workers and trafficked kids.

Despite all the backlash from individuals, including from NGOs who signed a letter to the organisation's board asking for the campaign to be taken down, or the coverage that persisted across several news articles, the organisation stood by their campaign. They stated that they had used paid models (children from their community) and stories to represent the types of situations they dealt with at their organisation. The question is though, did these children really understand what their images were being used for? Did the girl know that she was being labelled as a sex worker? With the increasing popularity of smart phones and Facebook in Cambodia (over 40% of the population are registered users[xix]), isn't it possible that someone in her village could have seen this photo and thought that she was a sex worker? This would have a detrimental impact on her life.

Many foreigners (and locals) participate in poverty tourism to understand poverty. While it does raise social awareness for poverty, it really isn't worth the intrusive behaviour into the lives of community members. Often, tourists take their photos, and a piece of dignity from the impoverished people, and move on with their lives. And for those who do choose to help those living in poverty, it can be gone about in ineffective ways.

Siem Reap is home to a rubbish dump called Anlong Pi. Every day, tourists visit this dump that is home to many Cambodians. Tourists take photos of the men, women and children who spend day upon day sorting through filthy rubbish just to make a couple of dollars.[xx] Not only does this intrude on the lives of these people who are simply trying to make a living, it also encourages the children to stay out of school, so they can perhaps make a few dollars from the tourists who are turning their lives into an attraction.

In 2016, I was in contact with a man from Italy whose service club had previously donated funds to Human and Hope Association. He was coming to Siem Reap and wanted advice on what to do. I gave him some suggestions, then told him that he shouldn't visit Chong Khneas in Tonle Sap, a major tourist trap that takes advantage of tourists, exploits children, and invades the privacy of villagers who live on the water.

IT'S NOT ABOUT ME

When this man visited Human and Hope Association a few weeks later, he told me that despite my suggestion, he had been persuaded to visit Chong Khneas. He, along with some travellers he had met in Siem Reap were taken on a boat tour of the lake. Whilst on the boat tour, they were taken to a shop on the lake and coerced by their driver into buying a bag of rice for twice the market rate. They were then taken to a local public school on the water, where the children at the school were waiting for them. This man and his friends donated the rice to the school and were told that the rice would be distributed amongst the children. While this situation is already not ideal, as the children are not afforded the opportunity of a real education with tourists rocking up all day and every day, the rice often isn't even given to the children. What sometimes happens is the boat driver or guide will come back later and sell the rice, then the money is split between them and the shop owner, and perhaps the teacher.

Chong Khneas is home to hundreds, if not thousands, of villagers who are trying to go about their normal lives without having their privacy invaded. There are numerous locals who take advantage of unsuspecting tourists, promote poverty tourism, and use unscrupulous tactics to earn a few bucks. There are numerous articles on the 'floating village rice scam' on the internet, from people who were, for lack of a better word, conned into buying rice for schools and orphanages on the lake. The issue is though, people continuously fall into this scam. My advice? Stay away from the place all together and do your best to not fall into the poverty tourism trap.

THERE ARE APPROXIMATELY 400 residential care institutions in Cambodia, housing over 40,000 children[xxi]. Despite what you would rightly assume about the children in these institutions being orphans, approximately 80% of them have at least one living parent[xxii].

Although the number of genuine orphans fell between 2005 and 2015, the number of orphanages increased by 60%.[xxiii] I think you know where I am heading with this; the opening of orphanages was fuelled by a demand from tourists and voluntourists alike. I myself visited an orphanage in 2009 after feeling a yearning to help poor, orphaned children; I volunteered at one and I came very close to working at one until I was told the true story of what went on.

It is a natural urge to want to help children without parents, however, these desires we have are creating a system where children are separated from their families and brought to orphanages to generate income from foreigners.

Many orphanages are run like businesses. They either buy or rent children from their parents or promise the desperate parents a better life for their children, which most of the time, isn't the case. These business orphanages are then often kept in bad conditions so that they can generate more income from unsuspecting tourists. Put your kids in the shoes of these 'orphans'. Would you want your children to grow up in an institution where visitors come day in and day out to play with them, take photos, and generally treat them like a tourist attraction? Do you know what the effect of orphanages on children are? Firstly, evidence shows that children, particularly those under the age of three, are at risk of permanent, developmental damage when they are not cared for in a family setting. They also often find it difficult to function properly in society when they eventually leave the orphanage. Children raised in orphanages are 10 times more likely to be involved in prostitution, 40 times more likely to have a criminal record, and 500 times more likely to commit suicide.[xxiv]

In late 2018, Australia became the first country to recognise orphanage trafficking as a form of modern slavery. More than 57 per cent of Australian universities advertise orphanage placements, and 14 per cent of our schools visit, volunteer or fundraise for these institutions, not to mention the number of individual travellers who visit and volunteer at them.[xxv] The harm that orphanages can cause are coming into the spotlight, however, the demand is still there.

On my latest trip back to Siem Reap, I was visiting a rural temple when I saw a busload of tourists pull up outside an orphanage adjacent to the temple. They were greeted by 'orphaned' children who gave them fruit, and I saw the cameras come out, with the tourists capturing plenty of photos of these vulnerable children. By the time I had finished up at the temple 15 minutes later, the bus was gone. This quick trip may have been seen as effective to the tourists, but the damage it did to the children can last a lifetime.

Instead of supporting orphanages, support organisations that are advocates for community-based care, ones that reintegrate children back into their families or are working to keep families together. As 'Orphanages No' advocates, breaking up families and institutionalising poor children is not the solution to child poverty.[xxvi]

ONE DAY IN 2016, Human and Hope Association was approached by a tour company in Phnom Penh. They wanted to bring 15 tourists from India to Human and Hope Association to *teach, play with the children and do something competitive* so that those tourists would have 'team building'. If we allowed them to do that, they would give us a donation in return.

I felt mortified. I had known that this was common practice with some tour companies, however, we had never been approached to partake in these crude activities before. Thai and I discussed this, and we decided he would phone the tour company back and explain that the community we work with needs stability, and that comes from the local staff who work with them day after day. Bringing a tour group in to play with the children is not part of our culture at Human and Hope Association, particularly as we did

IT'S NOT ABOUT ME

not accept foreign volunteers and have a strict policy for accepting Cambodian volunteers. Giving a tour of our organisation to this group wasn't even an option, as we have a rule that a maximum of five people can visit at a time to not overwhelm our villagers or make them feel like they are on show.

Thai phoned the tour company back and explained this. The staff member at the tour company understood our explanation, however, he then suggested that he could still bring the tour group and they would partake in activities with our staff, with us organising this. My blood started to boil. What was the point of this? Why would our staff take time out of their incredibly busy days to provide entertainment for a group of tourists? That's what it pretty much would be: entertainment. Instead of focusing on our mission, we were expected to play games and pretty much present ourselves as tourist attractions. Again, the offer of a donation was on the table.

Being a well-respected, legitimate organisation that strives to build the community around us, we stuck to our values and told the tour company that this wasn't possible. The sad thing is, despite our explanation of why this wasn't a good idea, I have no doubt that they would then approach other organisations or schools with the same request, and they would certainly find one who would say yes. During my time in Cambodia it became common practice for tourists to want to 'help' by partaking in something ineffective and possibly harmful, so they could feel good about themselves. I know of an NGO who was asked if *four hundred* tourists could come to their NGO and partake in 'team building'. This NGO said no, whilst trying to explain that not only was their organisation unable to host four hundred people, their community was, too. Think about it; four hundred people turning up to a small village? There would be road blocks, noise pollution, it would disrupt their everyday living, not to mention it would overwhelm the community.

The biggest thing I want people to get out of this book is that voluntourism and poverty tourism is *not* the correct way to interact with people in low-income countries. This way of thinking needs to be changed, and quickly. Tour providers, who typically strive to make their guests happy by organising such tours and events, should educate them on the pitfalls of treating children, and organisations as attractions. They should be protecting the vulnerable people in their country, not encouraging people to go and play with children they do not know, take photos and teach them things that local staff are more than capable of doing. They should not be dangling a donation with outrageous conditions that unfortunately some schools and NGOs must accept due to their financial situations.

Human and Hope Association, just like all the other charities and NGOs in the world, needs funds. There is no doubting that. However, we refuse to be a novelty for more fortunate people to play with. We are all human beings and we need to be treated as equals, not patronised by those who happen to be more fortunate than us.

'People want to know where their donations are going, that's why they want to visit and take part,' a friend once said to me.

'Why?' I responded. 'If an NGO is legitimate, they will have finances and reports readily available. They will have an up-to-date website, annual report and social media accounts. There shouldn't be a need for people to visit and take photos to ensure it is a good NGO. Do you see people who donate to the Cancer Council demanding to see their research facility in action before they donate? Isn't it strange that people would not do that in Australia, yet they feel they are entitled to in low-income countries?'

My friend couldn't help but agree with me. That point of view hadn't been presented to her before, as she was so used to being inundated with voluntourism opportunities, and had even just finished her own voluntourism stint, despite my advice. Attitudes towards low-income countries had to change and it started with us.

10. Creating Our Future

SITTING IN THE OFFICE one day, I started chatting to our volunteer, Thai, who had come in to prepare some documents before class. Thai was in grade 12 at public school and volunteered with us in the evenings after attending school all day. He would then drive a tuk-tuk after leaving Human and Hope Association so he could pay for his school fees. With his graduation just a few months away, I asked Thai what he was going to do when he finished school. He told me that he dreamed of attending university, but that he would need to get a full-time job that paid at least USD$80 a month in order to afford this.

My brain started going through the motions. Aside from being late a few times to class, Thai was an outstanding volunteer. He took his role very seriously, and from what I could observe from his teaching, he was great at engaging his students. I wanted to help Thai pursue further education, while also having him on our full-time team. Knowing that Heng was also eager to attend university, I contacted our main donor, and secured funding to provide both Thai and Heng with university scholarships for a four-year degree. I soon learned that another volunteer, Salin, was in the same situation as Thai and Heng. He was someone who I considered had great potential, despite some of his shortcomings such as being late to class, he was good at what he did. I knew that with support and encouragement he would thrive. And it is a chance I am proud that I took.

I went about drawing up the paperwork for a role for Thai as community liaison, which is a role we urgently needed. As we had slowly been increasing our daytime education classes, Heng and Chan had less time to commit to heading out to the community and building relationships with the villagers was crucial to our work. I once again put a call out to my networks, and my aunty offered to fund Thai's salary for a year, at a cost of USD$80 a month.

The director and I called a meeting with Heng and Thai, and I went about explaining that due to our belief in them, they were being awarded scholarships worth USD$2,000 for them to choose any degree and institution of their choice. We were also offering Thai full-time work.

They stared at us in disbelief, processing what we had just said. Their first question?

'Does this mean we work for the scholarship and don't get paid?'

'Of course not,' I responded, and gave them their contract, which included conditions related to their grades, their ongoing employment with Human and Hope Association, adherence with our code of conduct and a 'no marriage clause'.

We had consulted with another NGO that provided scholarships to determine what was expected from their scholarship recipients. The no marriage clause may seem strange to a foreign eye, but things work differently in Cambodia. Once you are married, you take responsibility for your partner's family. If you are working full-time and have the weight of two families on your shoulders, it is difficult to commit to studying (something that we saw happen with many villagers).

The guys, ecstatic that they were going to be attending university, couldn't wipe the smile off their faces. The photo I took of them that day, with their eyes shining, showed the hope they had for the future. Thai eagerly agreed to become community liaison once he finished high school four months later, and our team was brought to five.

And as for Salin? He was grateful when I told him about the scholarship, but it turned out he was only in grade 11. He would have to wait another year.

FROM MY INITIAL DAYS at Human and Hope Association, I had always planned to get a sewing program up and running. It was easy to get the team on board with this, as they knew that English classes weren't for everyone, and for those villagers who were over eighteen and hadn't finished school, sewing was the perfect skill. The great thing about sewing was that it was a skill that both men and women in Cambodia worked in. When driving through town, you would often see tailor shops with men sewing front and centre. There were no gender conformities with sewing.

To get funding to set up the program, I organised a fundraiser for my 27th birthday in early 2013. Sending out an email with the sewing program proposal to my family and friends, I pleaded with them to donate to my personal PayPal account, so I could purchase the initial materials required to set up the program. To begin with, we required five sewing machines, a cupboard, material, and the bits and bobs that were involved in sewing.

Once again, the generosity of those I cherished astounded me, and I secured the funds to set up the program. Before we were going to purchase anything, however, we needed to hire teaching staff who could then create the curriculum. I sought help from Sreylin, who had previously worked as a sewing assistant at another NGO, and she brought a candidate, *Champei, to help us. The idea was that we had two part-time teachers; one who taught in the morning, and one who taught in the afternoon.

The director and Heng interviewed the candidate and after celebrating the first employment interviews they had ever done, they decided we should hire Champei as our afternoon sewing teacher. Over the next few weeks, our team worked together to purchase the supplies we needed and work on a recruitment approach. We also hired our morning sewing teacher, Seyla, who came on as a recommendation from Sreylin and Champei.

After consulting with a Cambodian friend who ran outreach programs, we decided we would provide the students with a stipend of USD$15 a month for studying. This would encourage them to attend classes and help them meet their basic commitments whilst they took the time out to study. Feeling more confident after their recruitment of students for the preschool program, Heng and Chan headed out to our surrounding villages, and equipped with a survey to determine their level of poverty, recruited students for the program. We ended up with five morning students and five afternoon students who were all eager to study in the four-month program.

The day we came back from our Khmer New Year break in April was the day we launched the program. We held our breath until we saw that all the students had turned up, giving us hope for the success of the program. The students began by learning how to stitch on newspaper for the first few days, then eager to learn more, they made embroidered backpacks. The four-month program saw them making school uniforms for primary school students, in addition to tailored shirts for adults.

The first student to drop out was our only male student. He was a polite, young man who had learnt sewing very quickly. The problem was that his family needed him to be earning money straight away. They took out a loan and bought him a tuk-tuk, and told him he had to work immediately, so he left. After that, two other students dropped out with similar reasons.

We were left with seven students who were still eager to finish the program.

Nearing the end of the program, we presented the students with the opportunity to take out a microfinance loan to purchase a small sewing machine at a cost of USD$95. Surprisingly, only two students took us up on the offer. After assessing their personal situation and the ability to earn an income from the machines, we agreed to provide them with the machines which we purchased ourselves at the same shop where we had bought the machines for our classroom.

One of the students who took out a loan was Phalla. At the completion of the program, we hired Phalla to be the part-time sewing assistant to Seyla, earning USD$40 a month. At just 18 years old, Phalla had faced many challenges in her life. She had stopped studying in grade seven after the death of her younger sister; her mother had contracted a serious illness not long after, and as her older sister needed to take care of their mother, their income drastically decreased. Phalla could no longer afford to study, so instead she went to work at a restaurant full-time for USD$50 a month. When we approached Phalla to study in the sewing program, she jumped at the opportunity. Her commitment to sewing and her determined attitude was what made Seyla choose her as his assistant. Phalla worked in the morning, studied English at Human and Hope Association for an hour a day, and then made clothes for her neighbours in her spare time. Years later, she is still working at Human and Hope Association and has three sewing machines to her name.

The other student who took out a loan fell pregnant not soon after, due to a complicated pregnancy, gave up sewing. Although her machine went unused, she paid Human and Hope Association back the full amount and went on to sell the machine. Out of all of the semesters of sewing at Human and Hope Association, I believe the first was our most challenging, though I learnt a lot about the importance of involving the local community in the development of the program. Subsequent community collaboration enabled us to turn it into the thriving, life-changing program it is today.

WE WERE CONTINUING TO implement new projects at Human and Hope Association, but one project needed to go. Our volunteer, a former monk who had been teaching Buddhist studies every evening at 7pm, decided that he wanted to begin teaching the classes at his house instead. Due to our child protection policy, this wasn't possible, so we amicably decided to part ways. Whether he continued to teach classes at his house, I am not sure, however, it wasn't under our name.

We weren't a religious organisation (despite being located at a pagoda), and in the context of this teacher leaving it seemed the time to end the focus on Buddhism in classes. We updated our 'morality' curriculum and instead of referring to Buddhism in lessons, we steered towards a non-religious approach that taught the students topics such as money management, diversity, and problem-solving. A forty-week curriculum was developed, including lesson plans and resources. Each Friday, instead of English, the students studied these topics (that later went on to be named 'living values') and cleaned the pagoda for half an hour.

Things were plodding along well. Although the Australian dollar was continuing to drop, our funding was still consistent. Then, as always happens, a spanner was thrown into the works. One of our volunteers, Sokrithy, had told me he wouldn't be able to teach at Human and Hope Association anymore, as his family wanted him to earn more money. Once again, using the reactive approach that I was so used to in that first year, I scurried around to find funding, so we could hire Sokrithy on a full-time basis. We had wanted to introduce more classes and have a dedicated librarian, so this was the perfect timing.

Sokrithy could only be offered USD$80 a month, which his family felt wasn't enough, but with some persistence, he accepted the job offer, and our team became six.

The issues with some of our volunteers were still occurring, with volunteers being late to class or frequently absent. With no one to replace them when this happened, we were not providing consistency for our students, and they were falling further behind.

Two particular volunteers would be seen snapping at others, performing poorly with their teaching or not turning up to or participating in our weekly workshops. With a code of conduct and new policies in place to cement our expectations and values, it was time to take action.

One of the volunteers, Botum*, never appeared to be committed to teaching. It seemed as more of a social task for her, one where she could chat with her friends and share a common interest. Despite our best attempts to mentor her, she was often obstructive at our weekly workshops, and her behaviour was impacting other staff and volunteers. I raised this issue with the director, and he agreed that when the term was over, we would let Botum know that she would be let go. It was obvious what was happening; the volunteers with the most potential were being rewarded with employment, and the volunteers who weren't willing to improve, despite our encouragement, were no longer needed.

The term wasn't due to finish for another three months, so I asked the director to delay having the discussion with her until three weeks before the end of term. He ended up telling Botum about this the same day that we had the conversation. While I talked to the director about the further issues this could cause with Botum's teaching, he refused to take this on board.

The next day, I went to Australia, my first trip home in almost two years, with the situation playing on my mind. For the last couple of months, the director had been acting strangely. He was putting his personal relationships with the local volunteers over the wellbeing of Human and Hope Association and had a newfound attitude about him. Times were uncertain for me, and a trip home wasn't going to help.

NOW THAT WE WERE an official NGO, we could take the steps in Australia to set up an incorporated association. By doing that, we could take donations through an Australian bank account, and there would be no need for me to personally handle money anymore.

One of my friends who helped Human and Hope Association in the beginning with marketing and public relations was crucial in setting up the incorporated association. With me in Cambodia, there wasn't much I could do. She went about creating our constitution, getting pro bono legal help, and registering us as a charity. The day we were registered as a charity in Australia, 'Human and Hope Association Incorporated', was a happy day. When I returned to Australia for a holiday, I took professionally printed photos to sell, as well as handmade greeting cards by our art class students. A few contacts had offered to sell the cards, but in the end, we only received money for less than half. Some lost the cards, others were supposedly lost in the mail, and others gave up. It was another lesson learnt for me.

Now that we had fundraising licences in Australia, we could hold events! The first event was a trivia night in Adelaide, and the AUD$2,500 raised from that enabled us to hire two part-time security guards for Human and Hope Association. As there were some unruly characters who hung around the pagoda at night, and we were slowly increasing our inventory of sewing machines and computers, we needed to ensure everything was protected. Of course, unbeknown to me, one of the security guards we hired was the cousin of the director, and the casual security guard we hired was his brother. The nepotism was starting to show.

AFTER TALKING TO OUR education and library coordinator, Sokrithy, about the English school he set up in Kralanh, a district 60km from Siem Reap, I felt an urge to help.

Since Sokrithy's departure from the monkhood, the English school was being run by a monk, Venerable Borey*, and some villagers. Apart from Venerable Borey, none of the volunteers had great English. In fact, they were all at a beginner's level. This was because Kralanh was an area where education was lacking; being close to the Thai border, many of their community members left at a young age to work as builders in Thailand so they could support their families. It was an area that needed education the most, so the children would have more options to pursue when they were older.

IT'S NOT ABOUT ME

One afternoon on a public holiday, Sokrithy and I made the drive out to Kralanh to visit the Buddhist Foreign Language Association. It was a field trip to meet the local volunteers who were involved, take photos for fundraising, and to assess how Human and Hope Association could best help. Upon arriving at the pagoda, where it was based, Sokrithy took me around to show me the various places where they taught English. First was a wooden shack on stilts that I was afraid was going to crumble to the ground before my eyes. Then, across the road, was a similar shack, but made of bamboo. There was also an open classroom with desks, and a condemned building.

Sokrithy led me to the first classroom. He had called a meeting with the director and a teacher from the local public school, and his volunteers. They looked at me expectedly. I had no idea what they were anticipating. Then Sokrithy spoke up.

'They want you to say something in English,' he told me.

'Why?' I asked.

'Because they have never talked with a foreigner before.'

So, with that, I introduced myself as Sokrithy translated and the meeting attendees grinned at me.

Once that was over, they began talking about the future of Buddhist Foreign Language Association, with me catching every few words. With the safety risks of the current classrooms, Sokrithy's team wanted to teach at the local public school. Back in Siem Reap, I had suggested that we could provide the public school with library books each month as a 'thank you' for letting Buddhist Foreign Language Association use their classrooms after hours.

The director and teacher expressed their hesitations; apparently the Buddhist Foreign Language Association classes had been in there previously, and students had drawn on the walls. The team assured them that this wouldn't happen again, and in the end, it was verbally agreed that the classes could be held there. Success!

After we had said our goodbyes, I walked around with Sokrithy to take photos of the classes that were starting. It reminded me of Human and Hope Association just a few months prior; class sizes bulging at the seams, and little attention being paid by the students. I knew the teachers were doing the best they could, given their limited resources and the fact that they were teenagers themselves.

WHEN I RETURNED FROM our Pchum Benh break in October 2013, things were chaotic. The director and I were hardly on speaking terms, and I had no desire to be at work. Then, on the first day back, Heng told me that he had met a girl when he visited his homeland for three days during the break, and he had fallen in love and wanted to move back to his hometown and marry her.

'Really. After three days. Why?' I asked him.

'My heart beats fast when I see her,' he responded.

'Anything else?' I persisted.

'No,' he told me.

I proceeded to tell Heng that my heart beat fast whenever I saw a McDonald's, and although I thought it was great that he had feelings for this girl, he shouldn't throw his accomplishments away. He had a stable job at Human and Hope Association, was well into his first semester at university, and had some savings behind him for the first time in his life. If he were to move back to his rural hometown, he would lose it all.

Heng told me that he would think about what I said. I spent the night tossing and turning and hoping that he would make the right decision for his future. The next day, Heng told me that he was going to stay in Siem Reap. We dodged a bullet.

A couple of weeks later, another issue arose. Sokrithy was late to work, so I phoned him to see where he was. He answered the phone and told me he had an argument with his father and was moving to Thailand. He hung up, and when I tried calling him back, his phone was turned off.

I went to the office, in shock, and asked Thai what was going on. He told me I was best to replace Sokrithy's job at Human and Hope Association, because he wasn't coming back.

11. The Limitations of Life's Circumstances

IT IS A TERRIBLE feeling when you try with everything you've got to make a difference to better someone's life, but there are just too many factors in the way of them achieving positive outcomes. This happened more times than I could count in Cambodia. And the feeling of failure didn't subdue as time went on. I believe that every person should be treated as an individual and worked with in a way that suits their situation and personality. There is no cookie cutter approach to development, after all. But no matter how much passion and drive you hold to help someone, there can always be life circumstances that get in their way.

In early 2013, we secured funds to start a scholarship program at Human and Hope Association. Daily, we would see children playing at the pagoda when they should have been in public school. For varying reasons, they had not been enrolled by their parents or guardians. This meant that the children had no understanding of discipline, structure, and the importance of education. We wanted to help them, so with this scholarship program we were able to provide

IT'S NOT ABOUT ME

English education free of charge to the students and give them a study pack, so they had the materials they needed. A couple of our staff members headed out to the village where these children lived and convinced them to come to Human and Hope Association to study. It didn't take much convincing, as they were eager to receive free study resources.

The next Monday, 12 dishevelled-looking children ranging in age from seven to 13 came to class. We handed them plastic sleeves filled with books, pencils, and pens. The smiles on their faces were priceless. We showed the students into their classroom, and their learning began. The next day, only 10 students turned up. They continued to drop-out over the next couple of weeks until none were left.

We were relatively new to outreach, and our team were dumbfounded about how to approach the parents and guardians of the students, so we could bring them back to study. One boy, who lived in what I can best describe as an open bamboo shack, came back to study with us. He was seven years old, had lost his mother at a young age and was living with his father, who was unemployed. A shy boy, we started teaching him English. Though, as he didn't know how to read and write in his native language, he failed his class twice and had to repeat. We eventually convinced his father to enrol him in public school and offered them school uniforms made by our sewing students for a heavily discounted rate of USD$1. The boy began studying at public school and continued to attend English classes at Human and Hope Association, this time progressing. His confidence increased, but his behaviour worsened. He fell in with a group of children who demonstrated bad behaviour, started acting up and eventually stopped studying with us. With his father struggling to make ends meet, we hired him as a part-time security guard, though he was unreliable at best. However, he suddenly passed away, leaving his son an orphan at the age of nine. His son went to live with his sister, and as he was no longer a student of Human and Hope Association, there was not much we could do to ensure he stayed in school.

Another student from the initial intake of scholarship students was a girl aged 13. She was an orphan who lived with her grandparents who were trash pickers. Having never attended public school, this student was illiterate and spent her days picking up rubbish from the street to help put food on her plate. She stopped and started studying at Human and Hope Association more times than we could count, as she had to prioritise work over education, at 13 years of age. We always made exceptions for her, as she was living in extreme poverty, and we knew the risk of her being exploited into prostitution were high. One day, concerned about the number of lice in her hair, Heng asked her grandparents if we could get it shaved off. They agreed and hadn't done it themselves as they simply couldn't afford the USD$0.75 required to fix this situation. We paid to get her head shaved and enrolled her into our new Khmer language classes, so she could finally escape illiteracy. The deal was that when the new public-school year came around, we would provide her with a uniform and study supplies on the condition that she was enrolled in public school. Unfortunately, this student stopped studying with us before the school starter packs were distributed, so she didn't receive one. She, through no fault of her own given her volatile upbringing, hadn't been able to commit to studying. Months later, she began informally attending our library at our new location in Sambour Village. A few weeks later, she disappeared, and we never saw her at Human and Hope Association again.

My heart feels heavy when I think about the children who we couldn't help. I realised that we couldn't control every situation, and not only did the children need to be motivated to stay in school, their parents and guardians had to be supportive and see the value of education. These children and their families were living in extreme poverty, and it was only natural that they had to put survival first.

Although we tried hard, there is only so much time that our team can commit to following up with an individual. There are hundreds of people who use our services, and with only a handful of staff members, we make peace with the reality that some people have too many obstacles to overcome before they can commit. To this day, this still makes me sad.

SALLY HETHERINGTON OAM

AS A GENERAL RULE, you shouldn't become attached to the people you are trying to help. Sometimes, it is difficult not to. You tend to take a vested interest in someone because you see the situation they are living in, and know they deserve better. This is how I felt about three siblings, *Arun, *Bunroeun, and *Chea. These siblings lived near Human and Hope Association, and we would see them collecting trash on a daily basis. Aged between four and 13, the two brothers and sister were not in school. Their father sold bread with a mobile cart which he walked around in the mornings. Their mother took care of ducks at their home, and their eldest sister, 19, worked 12-14 hours a day at a food stall for a salary of USD$50 a month.

Arun and Bunroeun were the reason we began our Khmer language program in 2014. Heng frequently saw them on the road near the pagoda during school hours, and as he was worried about their futures, was compelled to help. He came to me and told me that teaching English to children who didn't know their native language was pretty much impossible. He wanted to take on the responsibility of teaching the two older siblings Khmer language. Inspired by his drive to initiate this project, I agreed this was the best way forward, so he approached Arun and Bunroeun's parents and promised to teach their children English and Khmer on the condition that when the new school year started, they would enrol them in public school.

IT'S NOT ABOUT ME

Their parents agreed, and Arun and Bunroeun joined daily Khmer classes with four other students. You wouldn't believe these two children had never attended school. They would always come to class early, treated their classmates and our staff with respect, and were incredibly committed to their studies. After class each day, they would spend time in our library, and on weekends they would attend art class with their younger brother. As time progressed, so did their knowledge, and when the new school year came around, Heng registered them. The issue was, Bunroeun didn't have a birth certificate. Only 73% of children under five years of age are registered as being born in Cambodia[xiii], and this lack of birth registration further exacerbates those living in poverty. A lack of birth registration contributes to children being unable to access education, health care and social welfare, and also makes them further vulnerable to exploitation and trafficking.[xiv] Although the public school agreed to let her into class, Bunroeun would face obstacles further down the track as having a birth certificate was a requirement of studying at public school.

We provided Arun and Bunroeun with school uniforms, study supplies, and with the help of another NGO, a bicycle so they could ride to school. On the first day of public school, they came to Human and Hope Association to park their bike (as they couldn't afford the five-cent parking fee at the public school) and ran all the way there. A short time later, they returned, having gotten their times mixed up. They were registered to study at school in the afternoon, not the morning! Seeing their excitement of finally attending school is one of the best memories I have during my time in Cambodia. Education is something so many people take for granted, yet this nine-year-old and 13-year-old grasped the opportunity as soon as it was presented to them.

We approached their parents about enrolling their youngest son, Chea, in our preschool program, as he had previously told us that he was four years old. As it turned out, he was seven, and small for his age. He should have been in our Khmer language program all along, and he should have already been attending public school. Heng jumped into action, and enrolled Chea in the same public-school class as Arun and Bunroeun.

Soon after, we moved to our new location in Sambour Commune. Arun, Bunroeun, and Chea studied in grade one at public school for half a day and came to Human and Hope Association for the other half to study English and Khmer. Fortunately, their months of studying Khmer with us had paid off. They thrived in school, with Arun coming top of his class, and Bunroeun and Chea in the top 10. Knowing that given his mature age, there was only so far that Arun would progress in school before he was forced to stop studying and work full-time, I asked Heng to talk with the director at Arun's public school and request that Arun skip a grade since he had progressed so much.

The request was granted, and Arun skipped ahead to grade three, whilst Bunroeun and Chea moved up to grade two.

Whilst all of this had been going on, we had provided a microfinance loan to the sibling's father, Dara*, so he could buy more ducks for his duck farm. This family lived in a shack on rented land, and their ducks were raised right beside their house; the odour and noise being quite unimaginable. We provided Dara with a budgeting workshop and provided a loan. All was going well, until the ducks escaped, and most were never to be seen again. We put a hold on repayments and worked with Dara to determine if he wanted to receive training from another NGO, so he could develop a skill. Given Dara had always been interested in motorbikes, another NGO kindly offered to train him in motorbike repairs. However, Dara, without explanation, decided he didn't want to learn motorbike repairs anymore. He went for work at a bakery for a month, then suddenly decided to quit. Another spanner was thrown into the works, with his wife finding out she was pregnant with her fifth child. She could no longer work as a trash picker, which put a heavier burden on the children.

The house of one of our sewing students.

Arun, Bunroeun, and Chea's attendance at both public school and Human and Hope Association started to dwindle as they had to take responsibility for supporting their family. Once the baby was born, Bunroeun, being female, stayed at home from school to look after the baby while her mother recovered then went back to work. Despite constant follow-ups from our team, there was nothing we could do to convince this family to allow their children to be educated. Their attendance dropped off from Human and Hope Association altogether, and their attendance at public school continued to be sketchy, at best. Bunroeun still didn't have her birth certificate to progress at public school.

On the day I left Cambodia, I saw Bunroeun riding her bicycle with a cart of rubbish attached to it. I cried a little and couldn't help feeling that I had failed her.

IT'S NOT ABOUT ME

As someone who grew up in a middle-class family, I found it very difficult to relate to the situations our community members were in. As much as I would love to think of myself as a compassionate and understanding person, not having lived in poverty myself, I had no first-hand experiences of the struggle to survive day-to-day. Despite knowing that education was the key to moving out of poverty, I didn't have a real understanding of the choices that our community members had to make. For some, taking time out to study would literally mean going to bed without a meal because of lost income, and this was something, despite living on a low income in Cambodia, I had never experienced. Although each person was unique in their circumstances, they all had a common context; having to make tough decisions in order to survive. As time went by, I came to realise that some people would never be able to move out of poverty because they were so far in debt, living in such dismal circumstances, or facing other challenges that were so difficult for me to comprehend that they would be living day-to-day for the rest of their lives. For a woman who originally thought she could save Cambodia, this was a stark realisation for me. I came to realise that although our grassroots approach to development was highly successful with the majority of people we worked with, we did have limitations when it came to what we could provide and what difference we could make to people living in such extreme, inter-generational poverty. That change could not come without greater support from the government and their policies, which was out of our capacity.

12. A Fork in the Road

TOWARDS THE END OF 2013, I was at my wits' end. The work I was doing to develop Human and Hope Association was constantly being overshadowed by issues with the director. The rest of the team were doing well; by that point we were a team of six full-time staff during the week, with Khmer volunteers running English classes on the weekends. But with the director being the one required to lead the organisation, I wasn't confident it would survive long-term.

We needed a leader who lived and breathed Human and Hope Association's values and would lead by example. There was a lack of accountability, nepotism was evident, and certain situations led to me and some members of our team not trusting him.

Two of our staff had heard from our students that the director had set up his own English school in our commune (but far enough away that we didn't realise). Every day, he would say goodbye to our team as he left early, and say, 'I am going to my course now.' And every day, he went to another workplace. The worst part was, he had recruited some of our students by offering them free education for the first month. Of course, once the second month rolled around the students didn't have the five dollars to pay, they came back to Human and Hope Association, which is how we found out what happened.

The director left in January 2014. When he found out we knew that he had broken our code of conduct, he resigned. I am grateful that this happened, as it allowed Human and Hope Association to move forward as an organisation. Had the director stayed, we wouldn't be where we are today.

On the day the director resigned, with a volunteer as my translator, we called a meeting. Our staff made their way to a classroom, with whispers going around wondering what the meeting was about. We had never called a meeting out of the blue before, and their intrigue was high.

'I have some news. As of today, the director is no longer working at Human and Hope Association. He has resigned.'

Everyone in the room was shocked. 'I do not want you to think of this as a bad thing. This is a fantastic opportunity for us to restructure our organisation and give our staff more responsibility. As of today, we are promoting several staff so there will be managers for each of our programs. This will enable us to develop our projects further. I will remain the operations manager and will work closely with the project managers to cultivate their skills. Then, at the beginning of next year, we will choose a new director from amongst the three managers who will lead the

IT'S NOT ABOUT ME

organisation. This is an exciting time for us, and I hope you are all ready to be part of some great changes in our community!'

Throughout my speech, our staff member, Thai, had remained very quiet, a distant look in his eyes. Out of everyone, the director's departure had affected him the most.

After the meeting was finished, I told Thai that we needed to take the director off the bank account, and he would replace him on there. We drove quietly to our bank, and my attempts at small talk whilst waiting for the teller were met with short answers. He was processing this all, and he needed time.

The next day, Thai came to work, ready for his new role as community manager. He had chosen to put the events of the day before aside, and was ready to move on, for the sake of Human and Hope Association. It is this determination and resilience that has led to Thai leading the organisation today.

IT TOOK THE DEBACLE of the director to realise that we didn't know anything about our constitution. Not wanting to risk him taking everything away from us, we looked at the copy, which was written in Khmer, and realised that it was completely incorrect. We also realised that, according to the document, Thai was deputy director, something he himself didn't know.

The team and I worked hard to write a new constitution and we made it into what it is today. Something we didn't have was a governing board.

Although we had one on paper, which included three volunteers who had left the organisation, this wasn't actioned in reality. In order to make changes to these documents and elect a new governing board from scratch, we needed the old governing board to sign the document. And with some of them having been dismissed, this wasn't going to be easy.

Thankfully, Thai was the type of person who didn't shy away from a challenge, so he went about collecting the signatures. First, was his cousin. Although he had been let go due to his unreliability, blood is thick, so he signed it. Another was a volunteer who had left on her own accord as she simply didn't have the time to commit. She also signed. Thai and Salin were on the board, so of course we had their signatures. But Davy, the first volunteer we let go, refused to sign it. She and her close friend, Sovann*, another former volunteer, told Thai that they wouldn't sign the document unless Human and Hope Association provided them with a reference. They were blackmailing us. And it once again made me breathe a sigh of relief that they were no longer on our team.

Thai told them that it was against our policy to give them references and left. Even without the signatures, he figured a way around it to get our document updated. He had saved the day.

Once the constitution was all written up, we needed to find a governing board. This board needed to be people we trusted, who were experienced in development and were committed to empowering our team. After brainstorming, we came up with a group of people who had already helped us in one way or another, and all but one had experience working at an NGO: A field coordinator, an accountant hotel, a production manager, a social worker and an English teacher. Thankfully, all five of them said yes when we approached them, and our constitution was signed.

It took Thai two trips to Phnom Penh and a USD$350 fee to update it. But we were now able to stay true to our constitution and go about our business with integrity.

THE FIRST HALF OF 2014 saw us initiate workshops for the community. The first was a resume writing workshop, which came about after I received resume after resume that weren't in the slightest bit professional. I wanted to ensure that our community were doing themselves justice. But that was the problem; I was focusing on what *I* wanted, not what the community needed. When it came to implementing the program, the only people who attended were university students who studied with our staff and lived in other communes. The people who lived in our target commune didn't have a need for resume writing workshops, as they were mainly self-employed or in trades that had no requirement for a resume. If I had asked the team to do a feasibility study, we would have understood this, and not wasted time and resources on a program that didn't have a positive impact on our community members. With an attitude of 'Sally knows best', I went in over enthusiastically with little thought. It wasn't the first time I had done this, and it was another mistake in my journey.

We also introduced successful workshops, including child protection for the students in our sewing program, so they could identify the types of abuse and report it if they saw it happening. The children in our education program attended our 'Good Touch, Bad Touch' workshops, and we also had a local women's centre run a workshop on rights in marriage.

Our education program was also developing, with a massive 89% of students passing their end of semester exams. After the director left, we made the decision to stop the weekend English classes, as our local volunteers often didn't turn up, leaving me to fill in, or the students to go without. The student numbers had also been dwindling, and we figured it was the perfect time to make the transition to a Sunday to Friday, 8am to 5pm opening. Although some students from the previous semester chose not to return, we did our best to accommodate those who wanted to. It had taken months to transition the class times from evening to day time, but it was for the best. Our evening students had complained of being harassed by monks and villagers at our pagoda on their ride home when they left class between 6pm and 7pm. The safety of our students and staff was very important to us, and we wanted to ensure our students were leaving our school while it was still light out, as many students had to ride their bicycles up to 4km home.

Also, the numbers in the evening classes had been dwindling, and there weren't enough students to justify holding classes, as we had a 10-student minimum and 18-student maximum rule. Thirdly, as most of our staff members were sponsored to study at university or English school, by this time, there was only one staff member who would be able to teach after 5pm, and with his limited English ability he could only teach the lower level classes that were held in the day time.

We also began opening our library on Sunday mornings for three hours, with around 15 to 20 students visiting the library each day. Our movie club, which focused on watching a movie and discussion time, increased in attendance.

WITH THE NEW ORGANISATIONAL structure running smoothly, it was time for me to concentrate on a project we had been aiming to launch the year before: a sewing business. The business would see us choosing the sewing students with the best quality work to make handicrafts at their home. They would be paid a fair wage, and I would be responsible for getting the products into stores. Although I had dreamed the previous year of having our own shop, I had soon come to realise that the overheads were simply too high for us to make a profit.

After consulting with the sewing teachers, we selected three of our advanced students to take part in the trial. They made a variety of handicrafts, ranging from simple eye masks to more complicated toy elephants. Basically, they were toys and accessories that I assumed would sell well in Siem Reap amongst the tourists. Once the two-month trial was finished, Chan and Thai sought feedback from the students and teachers on how the program could be improved. The only pressing feedback was that our orders couldn't be rushed, as they didn't want to feel pressured. They weren't working in factories, after all.

After lengthy discussions between Thai, Chan and myself, we decided on a format for the program. Firstly, a maximum of two students from each sewing class would be hired to be seamstresses. These students were to be classified as casual employees at Human and Hope Association and were required to follow our Code of Conduct and policies and procedures. In return, they were offered with participation in our staff savings scheme, holiday bonuses, inclusion in staff workshops and outings, and the ability to borrow machines through our microfinance program, interest-free.

We settled on a salary of 2,000 riel [USD$0.50] an hour, with a review to be conducted every six months. To ensure the seamstresses weren't reliant on us, we capped their salary at USD$70 a month. The sewing students gave feedback that the salary was fair, and they agreed there should be a maximum salary, so they would be motivated to fix their neighbours clothes; thus, they were not completely dependent on

Human and Hope Association and were empowered to make their own income.

At the end of the trial we hired two seamstresses, Navy* and Saney. Navy was a 23-year-old who grew up with four siblings. Although she was living in poverty, her life hadn't always been that way. Her family was classified as middle class, as her mother earnt a good salary as a teacher. Dependent on their mother, their world was rocked when she developed a serious illness and was unable to work. Navy's father was a soldier who lived off a small salary and was rarely in Siem Reap. When Navy's mother died, they had begun to live in extreme poverty.

Navy dropped out of school and helped her sister sell snacks so she could support her younger brother to continue studying. In the evenings, she was a dancer for tourists. A year after her mother passed away, Navy came across her mother's friends who encouraged her to go back to school. Since the director from the public school had known Navy's mother, he allowed her to enroll at school again. She went on to graduate and began volunteering part-time as a teacher's assistant at the local primary school, so she could gain teaching experience.

One day, the team at Human and Hope Association came across Navy when they were recruiting sewing students. She was chosen to study, and her efficiency and quality of sewing meant that she excelled in class. A year later, Navy resigned as a seamstress as she had secured a full-time teaching position at a private school in the city. Her job as a seamstress had been the financial stepping stone that supported her to achieve her dream of becoming a teacher.

The sewing business trial also made us aware that the machines we were providing the students with as part of the microfinance program weren't durable enough. They were having issues sewing thick fabric and requested that we sell their small sewing machines and take out an additional loan for the same machines that we had at Human and Hope Association. From that day, we stopped providing the small machines as part of the loans as we wanted to ensure we gave our students the best opportunity to earn money.

It was up to me to make the business profitable. This is where my experience running small businesses as a child finally came in handy! 'The Gazette', written, edited, produced and distributed by 10-year-old Sally, was a newspaper that had no predictable schedule. I would give TV show reviews, charge my mother, father and sister to put advertisements in for things they didn't care about, ask for feedback on certain issues such as whether Ross and Rachel were meant to end up together on *Friends* (spoiler alert: they were), and hold competitions. I would also use *The Gazette* to promote my other businesses like 'Sally's Show Bags', which was by far my most favourite. I would put my worldly possessions, such as my McDonald's Happy Meal Toys, into bags that were made from A4 pieces of paper stapled together. I would tape these bags to our dining room table, flip it on its side, and set up a booth that I thought rivalled the Royal Easter Show. My family were then able to purchase my show bags for between AUD$0.20 and AUD$1 each depending on the quality of the crap I put inside. However, there was one condition of purchase; they had to return it within the week. Although not very profitable, I still believe today that this was a valuable service offered to the community.

My business skills were so successful (in my mind, anyway), that I wrote a speech titled, 'How to make money when you are ten years old', which I entered into a public speaking competition. I walked away with 3rd place, though unfortunately there was no cash prize.

Setting up a handicraft business to ensure a sustainable source of income for Human and Hope Association was just the challenge I was looking for. We first approached a boutique hotel who agreed we could set up a stand in their lobby to sell our products. Chan and I went about buying a display rack, putting together an information sheet about Human and Hope Association, and then picking the best products to display. In the 10 months we kept our handicrafts there, we only sold one elephant. It wasn't the right market.

Soon after we placed the products in the hotel, I approached a contact who had a shop in an up-market hotel to generate income for her not-for-profit. Chan and I took samples to her, and she kindly agreed that we could put our products in her shop. In that first month, we made USD$44.50. The joy I felt when I picked up that cash hasn't left me today. I love making money, and to know that we were setting up something that would prove to be a sustainable source of income for the organisation long after I departed was thrilling.

Over the next few months, I approached shops and hotels that seemed to be aligned with our values. By the end of 2014, our products were in two hotels and six shops, and we were making a tidy profit every month.

WHILE ALL OF THIS was happening, our sewing program had been going through some major changes. After the first semester, we had realised that giving the students a cash stipend wasn't the correct way to go about things. Many of the students had husbands who drank a lot of alcohol, and we couldn't be certain whether that money was being used to provide nutrition to the families and schooling for the children, or whether it was being used for the grog. So, the next term, we changed the stipend to be a staple in every Cambodian's diet: rice.

For every day a student came to class, they would receive 1kg of rice to take home. Depending on the size of their family, this would cover just one meal, or the whole entire day. If the student didn't come to class, they didn't receive rice. It was a way to ensure they

IT'S NOT ABOUT ME

had food on their plates and motivated them to attend class.

In the second term of the program we once again began with 10 students, and by completion were down to seven. One student had stopped studying as she was Christian and didn't feel comfortable being at a Buddhist pagoda every day. Another had taken so much time off during the 2013 floods that she didn't have any desire to return. And the third had stopped as her family wanted her to get a full-time job.

Although it was disappointing every time a student stopped studying, we didn't let this deter us from continuing to develop the program. There was a special class of five women (including our seamstresses, Saney and Navy) who we had seen could take their skills to the next level. So, after bringing up the idea in a staff meeting, the team decided that we should start an advanced class, which would focus on university uniforms, handicrafts, and traditional ceremony tops.

Now that we were more in tune with the challenges that the students faced in their personal lives, I decided it was time to introduce life skills classes every Friday, just like the students in the education program studied living values. With a new program manager in place, he was responsible for developing the lesson plans and running the lessons, with the management of these classes eventually passed onto the sewing teachers. The life skills classes covered topics such as anger management, hygiene, and goal setting. Then, towards the end of the course, we went through resume writing with the students. As some were illiterate or had never held a job outside their homes before, this was a challenging task. Upon graduation, they were all given resumes, and with their knowledge on job hunting, were ready to go out and find jobs.

The thing is, they didn't want to.

All the women that were moving through the sewing program wanted to set up shops at their homes. Whilst we appreciated this ambition, the fact was that they all couldn't work from home; there were too many seamstresses already working in some of the areas where they lived, so they wouldn't be able to earn enough money to survive. It took us years to convince the students that working for an external shop or ethical factory was the best way to utilise their skill. By 2016, most of our students were securing employment working for others, as it had finally clicked that the income was so much better.

AT THE END OF 2013, we had planned to start a microfinance program. A friend of mine had raised the USD$1,500 we needed to begin the program, and one of our friends, Bora, who had previously run a microfinance program at a not-for-profit, had held a workshop for our team to help nut out the program. Although I was involved in the very early stages of the program development, by the time it came to implement the program, I had handed the whole program over to Thai.

We had identified that that was a need for the program as there were members of our community who did not have what was required to borrow money from a bank, such as literacy, a credit history and the willingness to take a bigger loan than is needed. Initially, we placed a USD$150 limit on the loans, though a few months later it was increased to USD$200 after we received feedback from the borrowers.

We advertised the program by posting announcements on trees, telling our students, and visiting the communities. The day of the initial information came in 2014 after months of planning, and anticipation was high. But no one showed up.

We waited. And waited. And waited.

Finally, forty-five minutes after the information session was due to begin, someone showed up. A few followed in the next thirty minutes. It was normal for Cambodians to be late, but our team had gotten used to punctuality, given it was one of our core values.

The information session began, and Thai and Salin provided the potential borrowers with the necessary knowledge related to the microfinance program and tips for business management. They then handed out application forms, and our team helped the borrowers to complete them. In total, three borrowers filled out forms. It was decided that one villager would not be provided with a loan as she simply had too much debt, and it was a high risk. We provided two loans; one to a woman who sold desserts at a stall on the side of the road, and one to a woman who had a food stall that we frequently bought our lunch from. They wanted to purchase furniture to ramp up the atmosphere for their customers and have money on hand for paying suppliers.

Before the borrower's loans were dispersed, Thai ran a workshop with them on money management and child protection. He then followed up with them every week when collecting the repayments. At first, things were going well for both borrowers. Then, one day, it all went downhill for one of them. This woman's landlord had become jealous of her success with her food stall (I can attest, she did make excellent fried beef), and evicted her so she could open her own food stall. The borrower, deflated, got a job in town and her dreams of being a small business owner were shattered. She still stayed true to her contract and paid us back every week until the entire loan was repaid. I refused to buy from the new food stall out of solidarity with the borrower.

The second borrower continued to have success with her dessert stall. She even took out a second loan, and business continued to improve. As time went by, our microfinance program began to expand due to word of mouth. We provided loans for flower sellers, livestock, vegetable sellers, shop owners, food carts, and carpenters. Thai made the decision to stop providing loans for livestock, as most of the pigs died and most of the ducks escaped, leaving the borrowers with no way to pay back their loans. Quickly, our 100% repayment rate went downhill. Borrowers didn't pay back their loans, and we were at a loss as to what to do. We didn't want to get the police involved, and we didn't have leverage to get the money back. Once, Thai was even chased off someone's property when he went to collect money.

A few years later, the microfinance was disbanded, and we dealt with our losses of several hundred dollars. To this day, I believe that one of the reasons it was unsuccessful is because the borrowers didn't have personal relationships with us; they didn't see what good we do for the community day in and day out, and therefore there was no urge to pay us back. Whereas our sewing microfinance program has maintained a 100% repayment rate since inception in 2013, since our students know and respect us.

13. A Distinct Culture

I RARELY VISITED THE community when I worked at Human and Hope Association. I was determined to leave that to our local, qualified staff who could speak the language, knew the culture and were there for the long haul. However, sometimes, for some reason or another, I needed to venture out there. It might have been because we were distributing sewing machines for our microfinance loans, or because I needed to take photos of our seamstresses. More often than not, it was because the male staff needed a female staff member to visit a community member with them. It would otherwise arouse suspicion (and jealousy) from the neighbours, husbands, and fathers of the people we visited if there wasn't a female presence. Given we didn't have any female staff in the office, that duty fell on me.

When I visited the community, I was confronted by the challenges that our villagers faced on a daily basis. It was different to when I sat in staff meetings, able to offer advice without emotions. When I was out in the community, I was no longer 'detached' from the issue, and it always reminded me of what dire circumstances some of our community were living in.

In 2014, I needed to go to a seamstresses' house to pay her salary for making our products. After giving the money to a very talented and happy woman (who then went on to start her own successful business), we headed to her friend's house.

Her friend had approached us to study in our sewing program. However, despite multiple efforts to get in contact with her, she failed to show up for her interview. Following the directions our seamstress gave us, we navigated the bumpy road to the woman's house, and I waited outside while my colleague went in to talk to her. He came back out a few minutes later with a frown on his face.

'She can't study. Her husband won't let her,' he told me.

Although this might seem hard to believe from an Australian perspective, this was all too common in Cambodia. The next week, six students began studying in our beginner sewing class. After just three days, an 18-year-old student dropped out. She really wanted to study, however, her husband, the same age as her, forbade it. The villagers and her husband's family told her husband that his wife should not study as there was no value in doing so.

'Study and no benefit. Work and have money,' they told her husband.

Two more students dropped out of that class, leaving us with just three students for the remainder of the year. When I am asked about the challenges of working with people who are living in extreme poverty, my response is the biggest issue we face is related to their families. Encouraging a family who hasn't had an opportunity to be educated to value education can be difficult. This happens most often in our sewing program. The first challenge to overcome is persuading the families to allow the students to study. I have lost track of the number of times that a woman has said, 'Yes, I want to study, but I have to ask my husband.' Most of the time the husband says no, and that is the end of that short journey. Or for the younger students, 'I really want to study as I stopped at public school, but my mother wants me to work and won't let me study.' Or, 'I have always wanted to learn this skill, but no one will look after my baby while I study.'

Despite having intelligent and relatable local staff who come from poverty themselves, no amount of talking can get those students to remain in the program; for them, instant results, such as money to help them make it through another day, is their first priority. If their families don't support them, they don't have a chance. What happens to them once they drop out of the program? Generally, they work as builders, move to Thailand where they are vulnerable to exploitation, or stay at home, thus remaining in poverty.

In 2016, I had reached my wits' end. It was costing a substantial amount of money to train these women in sewing, and every time a person dropped out of the program, our funding wasn't efficiently used as they didn't have enough skills to make a living out of it. I remained committed to investing in these villagers, but I knew that something had to change. After consulting with Seyla, our vocational training manager, and Salin, our education and community manager, we decided to reduce the duration of the program. Instead of three semesters at four months each, we changed the semesters to five months each and cut them down to two. The reasoning was that the students had to commit less time to the program, which would increase the likelihood of their families allowing them to study.

That wasn't enough, though. I knew we needed to implement a strategy to make our students understand what a big investment we were making in them, and how important it was for them to finish the program. My solution is what some might call extreme, but Seyla and Salin were on board, and it worked. We made a contract that stipulated if a student was to drop out of the program for reasons other than sickness or death of an immediate family member, they had to pay back Human and Hope Association 50% of what we had already invested in them. We didn't want their money, but this condition deterred villagers from signing up on a whim, or without the support of their families. It resulted in us recruiting the most committed villagers to join the program and stay in it. From that day, only one student has stopped studying prematurely in the sewing program, and she stayed true to the conditions of the contract. All the remaining students used their skill to earn an income after graduation.

I HAVE COME ACROSS many possessive men during my time living in Cambodia. Those men get jealous easily and seem to think that they 'own' their wives. Due to the way that many women are brought up, this seems normal and acceptable to them. One of our seamstresses used to tell our staff member, 'Don't phone me more than once, otherwise my husband will get angry and break my phone. But it is okay, because he loves me.'

In December 2015, just days before our team building trip to Preah Vihear, my colleague told me, 'Srey Pov* can't come on the trip anymore.'

'Why is that? She said she could before,' I answered.

'Her husband won't let her,' he replied. 'But I think that if you go and talk to him, he will listen to you.'

I doubted that he would listen to my reasoning, but I knew that if I went to her house, Srey Pov's husband would let her go on the trip. This is because foreigners were often seen as the ones that people should respect and obey. When I first joined Human and Hope Association in 2012, my colleague had proudly told me, 'The villagers like us now, because we have a foreigner here.' I felt there were so many things wrong with this, as I was always determined for local staff to be respected as experts by the community, since they *were* the experts. But misconceptions had made foreigners the ones who were to be revered by the community.

That day, my colleague and I headed to Srey Pov's house at lunchtime. I sat down with her husband, and with my colleague as my translator, we asked him why he wouldn't let his wife attend the team building trip. He wouldn't look me in the eye as he told me that there wouldn't be anyone to look after their daughter. I calmly asked him whether his parents could look after her, or a neighbor. He fidgeted and didn't speak for a while, then he agreed that yes, that could happen. The thing is, I knew he was lying to me. The reason he didn't want Srey Pov going on the trip was because she would be five hours away with other men, and he wouldn't have her in his sights. Fortunately, (or, unfortunately as I tend to look at it), I seemed to command some respect due to my white privilege, and Srey Pov's husband felt he had to let his wife go on the trip. This is the same man who she had to beg constantly to let her study in the sewing program at Human and Hope Association and is now proud of her since she often earns more than he does with her skill, resulting in them being able to build a new house.

SOMETHING I STRUGGLED WITH during my time in Cambodia was identifying whether to accept a situation as cultural acceptable or to challenge it. Although I wanted to ensure I was acting in a respectful way, there were some things I didn't know whether to let slide. Take for example the day I went out into the village surrounding Human and Hope Association in 2013. I had headed out with Heng and Chan, so I could take photos of their community outreach. It was while we were at the house of a girl who was about to start studying in preschool, that I came across something disturbing. While her mother was holding her naked baby brother, she kissed her baby brother's penis. I couldn't control my facial expressions, which could only be described as a look of distain, dismay, and distress. She, her mother, and neighbours looked at me and laughed, which is how Cambodians tend to handle awkward situations. I looked at my two colleagues and asked them, 'Is that normal?' They didn't have an answer for me. It made me realise the lines between cultural practices that border on being harmful and inappropriate. It is important to respect culture, but at what point should we be challenging it? This wasn't as confronting as genital mutilation, but in my Westerner's eyes, it was sexual abuse.

Torn up about whether this was something we should address, I contacted my friend, a foreign doctor who was in Cambodia for three years, training local staff at a hospital. She too, saw my predicament. Were we to accept it as cultural, or was this behaviour that the student had copied from someone else? Was she herself being abused? We decided to leave it, but the memory of that image couldn't leave me, nor has it left my mind today.

IT'S NOT ABOUT ME

A few months later, I ran 'Good Touch, Bad Touch' training for my team. The Good Touch, Bad Touch Project was developed as a way of communicating about sexual abuse and how to report it to school-aged children with culturally different backgrounds to my own in a creative way. Before our team was to roll it out to our students, Thai and I needed to run an all-day train-the-trainer session to fully equip them with the knowledge and to get them to understand why this topic was so important. At the start of the day, I brought up the situation I had seen months earlier, with the girl kissing her brother's penis. Nobody batted an eyelid. I then asked them if they pull on small boy's penises, which was also something I knew Cambodians did. Some of my colleagues looked down, ashamed to speak, as deep down, they understood it wasn't right. A Khmer volunteer at the time put up his hand and told me that he does it for fun.

I walked over to him and asked him, 'How would you feel if I pulled down your pants now and wrenched your penis without consent?'

He and the other men in the room flinched and admitted that it wouldn't feel good.

'So,' I challenged them, 'Why do you think it is acceptable to do it to children?'

They didn't have an answer, although I know from that day forward a few of them changed their behavior on that. Still, I am left wondering, is it something we should accept as cultural, or is it child abuse? I always wonder if I should have challenged people's actions more.

CAN I GET A holler from my sisters who have endometriosis? It is not easy dealing with the two weeks of PMS. Or the constant backaches. And headaches. And vomiting. Or the feeling that a knife is scraping against your uterus for three days. Oh, and who can forget the mood swings. It is even harder dealing with it in a country that likes to pretend that periods don't exist.

In Cambodia, periods are a taboo topic. Many women don't know anything about the purpose of periods, or how to maintain proper hygiene, as they rely on information from their mothers, who may have received incorrect information themselves. In Cambodia, women are told not to shower regularly during their period, as it is believed to affect the beauty of their skin. They are also told not to eat sour foods and fermented fish, as that increases the smell. Ice water and coconut juice is believed to block menstruation, so those are off limits, too.

For the first 14 months of living in Cambodia, I only had access to a bicycle. Riding a bicycle to work, to the grocery store and to hang out with friends was great exercise. However, when it came to that time of the month when I had my period, I couldn't bear to hop on. A journey that normally took me five minutes would take me 10. If I ran out of pads, I would have to ride 15 minutes into town to purchase them from the

IT'S NOT ABOUT ME

'Western' grocery store and avoid eye contact with the person at the cash register who was secretly judging me for being a woman.

When I bought a motorbike, travelling whilst on my period became a more pleasant journey, though my pain wasn't alleviated. I would drive my motorbike hunched over, nose scrunched up, body swaying back and forth to cope with the intense pain. But nothing helped.

Since the pain wasn't subduing, I decided I needed to be very open about my period with my mostly male workmates, so they could understand the reason I was more impatient than usual once a month. Every month, I would tell them that my period had arrived and explained the symptoms with them. Well, half explained, half cried. For a couple of years, they would shy away (or sometimes, run away) from the conversation, not believing that this Australian girl was openly talking about the blood that was coming out of her. However, I persisted. Periods, as unpleasant as they are, are a normal part of life. The fact is, my workmates wouldn't have been born without their mothers having their periods, so they needed to suck it up.

Eventually, I got through to them.

Me: 'I am getting my period.'

Salin: 'Okay, stay home tomorrow.'

Heng: 'I now understand about periods. They are so bad. When my future wife gets her period, I will make her rest for three days.'

Me: 'I have stomach pains. Am I getting my period?'
Met*: *Looks at watch* 'Yes, I think you had it one month ago.'

Hearing about my period became such a normal part of life for my team, that when I suggested we include period education in our sewing classes, and Khmer books about periods in our library, they didn't resist. They welcomed this addition and agreed that it was important to educate the community about periods, feminine hygiene, and women's health.

And, to keep up with routine, I still email them once a month to tell them I have my period.

MONKS ARE REVERED AND treated with the utmost respect in Cambodia. When I was a tourist back in 2009, I stared at monks with intrigue, wondering what it was like to dedicate your life to Buddha. They seemed like such a mystery to me. Many young Cambodian boys choose to become monks because they are living in poverty, and this is a way for them to access shelter and food. Others join because they are genuinely interested in learning about Buddhism. Whatever the reason, becoming a monk comes with sacrifices; they must live regulated lifestyles, with over 200 rules to follow. These include not touching or having an ill-mannered conversation with a woman, not to lie, and not to consume foods between noon and the following dawn.

When people think of pagodas, they usually think of a quiet, clean place that is dedicated to worshipping. The pagoda we were at was anything but. When I first started working at Human and Hope Association, I was fascinated by the monks. As time went by, I became concerned.

Not all monks demonstrated poor behaviour, but I can honestly say I saw more than a handful at this pagoda break the rules they were bound by. One monk had a girlfriend, which was forbidden, and would spend hours playing tonsil hockey with her on the pagoda grounds. One of the older monks kept the big speakers for ceremonies in a room in our building, and he would often lock himself in the room and listen to modern music, which was also forbidden. Another monk told me he loved me.

We were told that the monks were starting Sanskrit classes, and they needed to use a classroom. The school building that we were in had originally been built for these classes, but nothing had come out of it. We vacated the classroom and adjusted our timetable, so we would no longer need that room. Yet it went unused for months. We found out the room was only there so if a district pagoda committee turned up, they could 'show' that they were teaching Sanskrit. It was all a big lie.

Once, when I was in Heng's room practising my Khmer at lunch, two of the monks I was friends with came inside. One sat beside me, helping me read, whilst the other sat directly in front of me. I suddenly felt a jerk on my left big toe. I screamed and looked up. The monk had pulled my toe, and was sitting there, smirking at me. Touching females was forbidden, and he was playing with fire. I began telling him off, then Heng shushed me,

'Sally, if the villagers find out, it is you they will blame. They will say you encouraged him,' he told me.

Feeling violated, I left the room. Following that day, that monk would call out to me and flex his miniature muscles like he was in a bodybuilding show. He would laugh, and I would cringe.

Monks were supposed to be role models to our students and the community, but many of the ones I came across at that pagoda were far from it. For years since leaving that pagoda, I have reflected on the power that monks have. They are held in the highest esteem, and with 95% of the Cambodian population identifying as Buddhist, that is many people who support the pagodas where the monks live. Most days, I would see monks returning from ceremonies with new robes, food, soft drink, candles, and money. Cambodians who were struggling to eat would give away what little they had to the monks, as they dreamed of being reincarnated into a better life.

What I came to realise was that these monks were, at the end of the day, humans. They have weaknesses just like everyone else, and many had joined the monkhood to survive. I sympathised with them at the same time as being uncomfortable with the behaviour they were demonstrating. I would often think to myself that they were disrespecting their religion and the community who worked so hard to provide for them when they broke the rules. Yet, the community continued to support them because it was so engrained in their culture.

I could live in Cambodia my whole life, and I would never entirely understand the culture; it isn't in my blood, nor did I grow up with it. And that is the biggest reason why it is important for the Cambodian team at Human and Hope Association to run the organisation; they know the culture of their community, and they can make the right decisions on whether they should be challenging it.

14. Time for a Change

WARNING: This chapter contains upsetting child sexual abuse content.

I WAS SITTING IN the office when I heard crying outside. Walking outside to investigate, I looked around the balcony, in the library, and both downstairs classrooms. Nope, no crying child to be seen. I then walked upstairs, and heard the crying get louder. Walking towards the sewing room, I saw one of our students standing outside the classroom, looking over at the pagoda.

'Sally,' she told me in Khmer, pointing towards the pagoda. 'Teacher Thai told us that isn't good.'

What wasn't good? I kept hearing the crying, but I had no idea what was going on. At that moment, the sewing teacher, Seyla, came out and told me that the crying was coming from the pagoda; there was a small boy there with his pants down, and some monks and villagers were taking photos of his genitals.

'*What?!*' I exclaimed, as I marched away from the sewing room, anger boiling inside of me, and a hunger for justice.

IT'S NOT ABOUT ME

I ran down the stairs of our building and walked past the classrooms where Heng and Chan were standing outside, also looking over at the pagoda.

'What they are doing is wrong,' I told them in a raised voice.

'I'm going to stop them! Will you come with me?' I asked.

Heng looked at me. 'I can't come. In our culture, we can't say the bad words to monks. And because I live here, it will cause a big problem for me.'

I looked at Chan, and he shrugged his shoulders sheepishly. As it later turned out, one of his cousins was an offending monk.

Determined not to waste any more time, I continued my march past our office, down the steps and across to the pagoda. Boy, did those monks and villagers see me coming.

As I walked up the stairs of the colourful pagoda, I looked to my left and saw a small boy, his face wet and red, with his pants pulled down. He was a former student of ours, a gentle and sweet boy that I had always enjoyed playing games with.

I turned back to the two monks and villagers, and told them in my broken Khmer, 'Stop. Stop it now. Give me your phones.'

One of the monks, who had been identified as verbally harassing our students over the previous months, handed me his phone. I flicked through the photos but didn't find the photos of the boy. Whilst I was doing that, I realised that Seyla was behind me.

He had followed me on my march and had made his way to the boy and pulled up his pants.

I thrust the phone back at the monk, then saw that one of the villagers had been going through his phone whilst I was looking at the monk's phone. He had been deleting the photos.

Having already used up all the words I knew in Khmer, I began speaking in English, with Seyla translating.

'What you have done is very bad. It is not okay to do this to anyone. If you ever do it again, I am calling the police,' I said to them, sternly, as they stared at me with part hate and part amusement in their faces.

As Seyla translated, he added some extra words to try and get the monks and villagers to understand that this was classified as child pornography, and it was illegal. Not wanting to be near them a minute longer, I gently took the child by the shoulders, and speaking calming words to him, took him back to our office.

I sat him down and asked a staff member to look after him while I phoned Thai, who had been out on a community visit, and requested that he return to Human and Hope Association. While the child eventually calmed down, I didn't. Here we were, hosting hundreds of children at our school each day, and there were people we couldn't trust, including the monks, just a few feet away from us. How could we ensure the students were thoroughly protected when they came into our care? How could we make sure this didn't happen again?

My comment about calling the police had been a bluff. I knew they wouldn't do anything about it, and I assumed the monks and villagers knew that, too. I felt powerless.

Thai soon returned, and after explaining what had happened, he took the boy home. He encouraged the boy's mother not to let him come to the pagoda unaccompanied, but it was just a few short weeks before I saw him back there again.

Thai went to the head monk and explained what happened and offered to hold a child protection workshop for the monks so that they could understand what acceptable and unacceptable behaviour was. The head monk just brushed it off and said there wasn't an issue. The offending monks steered clear of us after that day.

THAT INCIDENT WAS THE push we needed to move. Just days earlier, Thai had told me that the pagoda committee were talking about stopping their rental of the building to us. The old director's relatives were on the committee, and we had heard through the grapevine that he was saying bad things about the organisation. At first, I thought we couldn't afford it. But after this incident, I knew we couldn't afford not to.

Thai, Heng, Chan, and I met to discuss a plan of action. We knew we had to move, and we had to do so quickly and in the cheapest way possible. At first, we thought we should buy land. But then we realised that an individual's name would need to be attached to the land ownership, and no one wanted that responsibility out of fear that we would assume they would then go on to sell the land. Besides, the land prices were skyrocketing in Siem Reap, and we simply couldn't afford it.

We then decided that renting land was the way to go, and we could build our own community centre, the way we wanted it. We spent the next few days driving around the villages near Human and Hope Association, trying to find land rentals, but didn't have much luck. Then I had a thought.

'A few months ago, I drove out to Sambour commune to take photos of the pagoda. I was struck by the poverty that people out there are living in. It is so much worse than our community,' I told Thai, Heng, and Chan one morning.

It was like a light bulb had gone on. Each of the three guys talked about how they also knew Sambour commune was lacking the services we provided and given that some of our students were already making the 8km round journey by bicycle from Sambour each day, they knew we could still service this area if we moved to Sambour. After further discussions, we made the big decision. We were going to vacate the pagoda and build our own community centre in a rural area where, according to commune data, the poverty rates were much worse.

We flew into action. As this was a delicate situation, and we didn't want to risk getting kicked out of our premises before we secured the move; we were keeping this move between the four of us for now.

We took turns driving to Sambour commune and trying to find land. When we came across the perfect piece of land, we were left disappointed after the owner wouldn't rent it, she only wanted to sell it. A year later, that strip of road became overdeveloped, and I knew it was for the best that we didn't get it.

While this was going on, I was busy managing a crowdfunding campaign, so we could secure the funds to move. Our Australian fundraising partner, which I was on the board of, managed to raise enough funds to start the build; and this was even without the offer of tax deductibility, which we didn't secure until the end of 2014. As the money continued to trickle in, we continued to look for the place that we could call our home.

One afternoon, when I was in the office, I got a call from the team.

'Sally, we have found a place. It is very good, and it has a house on it. But it is USD$300 a month,' I was told.

'That's not within our budget, but I will come and have a look anyway,' I responded.

I hopped on my motorbike and rode down the main road until I saw one of the guys step out and wave to me. I pulled my motorbike over into overgrown grass and looked around. The land was *huge*. It had a house in the right-hand corner, and was a big area filled with long grass, a few trees and a cow munching on his afternoon snack.

We got talking with the landlord, and I told him we couldn't afford the rent. But what about if we cut the land in half, then he could rent out the house to someone else, I asked.

He thought about it for a while. Some rent for the time being was better than no rent. He agreed with my suggestion, and offered to bear the cost of the fence. I liked this guy!

'We would like a land contract of twenty years,' I told him, referring to the previous conversation where we had all decided that a twenty-year lease would enable us to move a generation out of poverty.

'I can't do that,' the landlord shook his head.

'How long can you do?' I asked him.

He thought for some time. 'I can do 15 years, but the price must increase every five years. USD$130 per month to begin with, and then it goes up.'

The team and I discussed this offer.

'We'll take it,' I said.

Determined to do this thing right, and not risk getting stiffed by the landlord, which often happens in Cambodia, we found a lawyer and paid him four hundred dollars to draw up contracts in English and Khmer stipulating our conditions. Thai and I signed on behalf of Human and Hope Association, and our kind landlord gave us three months' rent free of charge while we built. This was it. We were building our own community centre!

IT'S NOT ABOUT ME

I DREW UP A plan (albeit, a very basic plan) on paper with what the school would require. Considering our basic needs, it included three classrooms, a combined office and library, a sewing room, play area, one toilet, and a storage shed. Right in the middle of the plan I included a study area, so our students could have a large, safe place to study outside of class. The team wanted a volleyball court, but my justifications for a study area soon won them over.

Included in the plan was a farm. We were serious about earning our own income, and now that we had land that we could do whatever we wanted with, this was the perfect opportunity to reduce costs and make some profit. The farm would be used to grow chemical-free vegetables to be used for our staff lunches and art class snacks, with the remainder to be sold to local market vendors. We would also have a section for the sewing students to have their own farm to take care of. This would enable us to provide them with fresh vegetables as part of their stipend two days a week, reducing the cost of rice.

We needed a builder we could trust, so, with Thai abstaining from the vote, we decided to hire his father to be the project manager for construction. Finally, with enough funds to start building the basics, it was time to tell our team about the move. We called a meeting one afternoon (the second special meeting we had held that year) and explained the move to our team. Our seamstresses were over the moon, as they lived in Sambour, so it meant less travel for them. As for our other staff, we promised a petrol allowance, so they wouldn't be out of pocket for the extra travel.

We then notified the monks that we would be vacating the premises at the end of October, to coincide with the new term, so we didn't disrupt our students learning. When we told the students, there was a mixture of reactions. Some were committed to making the move with us, but many weren't. The journey was just too far for them on that dangerous road.

Construction began, and with money still coming in here and there, we were able to add extras; a preschool classroom, a second toilet, and paint to the walls. Within three weeks, the community centre was built. But the issue was, it was a complete mess. The builders hadn't cleaned up, so that responsibility was on us. Our staff, sewing students and board members spent a few Saturdays, our only day off, working to bring the place up to scratch. We cut the grass, scrubbed the floors, gutted the ponds, planted vegetable seeds, painted chalkboards, laid down gravel, and decorated the place. With a lot of hard work, we were able to stay on schedule for the move.

The weekend we moved was possibly the most exhausting of my life. After we had spent weeks packing up our belongings from the pagoda, we spent the Friday afternoon and Saturday moving and putting everything in place, ready to start classes on the Monday.

For one month leading up to the move, our education team had been driving around Sambour and telling the villagers about our programs. We had over one hundred students register for the English program, so to keep them engaged before the move, we started daily classes in the study area at the new location. Each day, a teacher and I would hold art class and promote our core student values. We were still running our education programs at our old location, so resources were tight, and time was valuable. But we made it work because we believed in what we did.

In the end, it cost us USD$20,000 to build our community centre. We had provided jobs to 15 local builders (including the parents of our poorest students), purchased all our resources locally, and utilised hundreds of hours of volunteer time by Cambodians. We had turned this all around in six months.

THE BIG DAY HAD finally come. After months of dedication, we were finally opening our very own community centre. A place that would be ours for the next fifteen years. A place that would welcome thousands of villagers and empower them through our projects that were achieving great outcomes. A place where our students would be safe.

With our team, students from the pagoda, community partners, and villagers, we celebrated our move to Sambour. For weeks, I had been practising a speech in Khmer, which was overshadowed by a patchy microphone. When I asked our teacher, Met, if he understood it, he told me he didn't.

Approximately one third of the students in our education program followed us to Sambour. By the beginning of 2015, this had been reduced to eight students. And by the middle of 2016, none.

15. Superstition and Ghouls

I'M GOING TO PUT this out there. I am terrified of ghosts. I wish I were a sceptic, but I am afraid of the unknown. The first time I saw a ghost was when I was eight years old. I was heading to bed for the night and doing that; I needed to walk down a dark hallway past two bedrooms to get to mine. As I was walking past my sister's bedroom, almost at the home stretch, I saw something white hovering out of the corner of my left eye. I gasped, and tailgated it back down the hallway, where I grabbed my father. Too ashamed to tell him I thought I saw a ghost, I grabbed his hand and asked him to walk me to my bedroom, but first to stop at my sister's room and turn on the light. He obliged, and when he turned on the light, nothing was there. I suppose it could have been my imagination or a flash of light. However, a part of me still wonders to this day if it was a ghost.

My second and only other experience with a ghost was in 2008. New to Sydney, I had been invited on a ghost tour with some colleagues, so despite my fear of ghouls, I accepted. After all, I wanted to make friends with my work colleagues.

The tour took place in The Rocks, near Circular Quay. It was eerie; however, I didn't see or feel any ghosts. That is, until the end of the tour. We had ventured into an excavated house, previously tenanted by numerous families over a couple of centuries. As we were standing in the cold, still air, I felt someone tickling the right side of my neck. I quickly turned around to see who was attempting to scare me; then I realised that nobody had been standing close by at all. I hadn't been tickled by a human. I was glad that was the final stop on the ghost tour, as I didn't want to get close to any more ghosts.

Those two experiences were the only times I had come close to the supernatural. That is, until I moved to Cambodia.

CAMBODIA IS A SUPERSTITIOUS country. My partner doesn't like to step over me, as he says that if he does that, I will fall pregnant. It is a thought that if you sing whilst cooking, you will marry someone who is widowed or divorced. If you watch two dogs having sex, you will contract an eye infection. If you grow lemongrass with the bottom up, you can stop the rain. If a duck flies onto the roof of your house, you will have bad luck. If you dream about a snake biting you that won't let go, your soulmate will arrive. If an eclipse occurs whilst a couple is engaged, the woman must go and live at the man's house, or they will have many difficulties during the marriage.

IT'S NOT ABOUT ME

Although I laugh at these, I have come to adore this charming part of Cambodia. I also can't help but wonder if some of these superstitions are in fact, reality. I saw dogs having sex during my time working at the pagoda, and often had difficulties with my eyes in Cambodia. Perhaps it was just the dirt and dust, but you never know.

A few weeks before finishing up at Human and Hope Association, we were searching for a new sewing teacher. I wanted to ensure that the sewing program was reaching its full potential before I departed, as I saw it as my 'baby', and we had invested so much money each semester into it. The person I had my eye on for the job was a sewing graduate who was working as a seamstress for Human and Hope Association, making handicrafts at her home. Chomrong was a year older than me, with three children and a husband living in an unstable bamboo and straw house. Every time I climbed the creaky wooden stairs into her house, I was convinced death was upon me.

Chomrong was an incredibly intelligent woman who was never afforded the opportunity to study past grade eight. Her children had inherited her intelligence, and two of them were studying at a public school in addition to Human and Hope Association, whilst her youngest stayed at home with her.

I knew Chomrong was the right person for the job, as she was a no-nonsense kind of woman. She accepted feedback, would speak up when things weren't right and was the best role model for the women coming through our program. When our team approached her to apply for the role, however, Chomrong had excuses. Although she was keen to put her name forward for the role, she had a problem. Her cow had five nipples.

You see, when cows are born with five nipples, they are not allowed to be killed. The belief in Cambodia is that if you kill a cow with five nipples, you will become poor. Chomrong, a very intelligent woman (I can't stress this enough), needed to spend her time walking her cow and looking after her. If she worked at Human and Hope Association, she wouldn't have time to look after the cow. If she sold the cow to be killed, she would be poor forever. The irony is, however, that she was already poor, and keeping the cow instead of taking up permanent, well-paid employment would keep her in poverty.

I was exasperated. Whilst I am completely supportive of cultural beliefs, I just couldn't believe that Chomrong would give up this incredible opportunity based on a superstition.

A couple of weeks went by, and we didn't come any closer to finding a replacement sewing teacher. Then one day, Chomrong had a change of mind. Her husband told her that he would take care of the cow, so she could work, and Chomrong approached us for an interview. She was hired and now has a permanent part-time job at Human and Hope Association in addition to making our handicrafts at her home. She and her husband have built a new brick house, and have moved out of the poverty bracket.

IN FEBRUARY 2013, WHEN I was still new to Human and Hope Association, I saw a ghost.

I had been working in the office when, as often happened, I had an overwhelming urge to pee. I walked out of the office, along with the balcony and after jumping down a couple of steps, turned left to reach our toilet. After squatting to do my business, then running water over my hands from the basin, I opened the door and stepped outside. I looked towards the back of the building to the right, where a cement fence with small pillars stood. There was a small boy, only reaching half the height of the fence, with his arms by his side standing pressed against the wall. I glanced left, then quickly looked back to the right, and the boy was gone.

I immediately ran away from the toilet and reached the office in a matter of seconds. 'I saw a *ghost,*' I cried out to the director and my friend who was there at the time. I quickly recounted the story, then looked out our office window at the wall. The ghost boy still hadn't reappeared, and I was left wondering what the hell had just happened.

Years later I learnt that the pagoda had been used as a prison during the time of the Khmer Rouge, with many people slaughtered within the pagoda walls. To this day, I wonder if that boy was a victim of the horrific slayings.

He wasn't to be the last ghost I saw in Cambodia.

THERE IS A BELIEF in Cambodia that when a person dies, they wander around the village as a spirit until the proper rituals have taken place. If the proper rituals are not performed, the deceased will not be able to move onto their next life.

When a person dies, the family brings the body home and washes, dresses, and places it into a coffin. Dissection or removal of the organs is a big no-no, as this would affect the rebirth of the deceased person. From the very first day of the person dying, a ceremony is held at the deceased's house. Villagers will come and give money to the family, pray and eat food. For the next three days, the body remains at the house, and that is when creepy things happen.

The neighbourhoods I lived in were quiet, apart from the chickens squawking in the early mornings, and the occasional fight between husband and wife. Once every few weeks, however, this was a different case. The dogs in my neighbourhood would go rabid in the evenings. For hours on end, they would bark mercilessly, to no avail. I would have many sleepless nights in a row, and I never understood why.

Until one day, a colleague explained to me that the reason the dogs were barking so ferociously was because someone had died, and their spirit was wandering around aimlessly until they were to be cremated. It made sense, as strange as it may sound to some people. From then on, I made a conscious effort to listen out for funeral music in my neighbourhood. And you can be guaranteed, every time there was a funeral, the dogs at my house and in my village would be barking all night for three nights.

After those three nights are over, a funeral procession is held to carry the body to the pagoda for cremation. Hundreds of people walk down a road, stopping traffic, with the coffin placed on a moving vehicle surrounded by monks. Once the group arrives at the pagoda, the coffin is cremated, usually by shooting an arrow with fire at it. The cremation is believed to allow the soul of the deceased to part from the body and go to heaven or hell while they wait to be reincarnated. And after that, the nighttime barking stops. Until another person dies, which was quite often.

'DO YOU WANT TO share what you are talking about?' I asked my student who was chatting with her friend instead of concentrating on her worksheet.

'Teacher, I am telling my friend about a girl in my village who died.'

'Oh, I am sorry to hear that. How did she die?'

'She was in the hospital and was sick, and then she died. And then they brought her body back to her house for the funeral, but she woke up.'

'She was dead; then she wasn't dead?!'

'Yes, so all my villagers came and looked at her. She was so hungry, she ate a lot of food, and she slept a lot.'

'That is incredibly creepy,' I said, and went back to teaching.

A couple of days later, I asked my student how the girl was doing.

'Oh, she died again. We had the funeral for her.'

I will never know if this was the work of the supernatural, or if she was mistakenly pronounced dead in the first place. Both scenarios terrify me.

I USED TO VOLUNTEER once a week at an English school near Angkor Wat. It was my job to develop a conversational English curriculum and then teach the students, aged between 14 and 24.

It was too far to ride to Angkor Wat after my full-time job as volunteer coordinator every week, so I used to ride my bicycle into town and lock it. I would then switch from my bicycle helmet to my motorbike helmet and jump on the back of a motorbike and head to their office about 3km from town. The Khmer teacher at this organisation would then drive me on his motorbike to the school, and after class finished, would drop me back in the town where I would breathe a sigh of relief every time that my bicycle was still there.

To get to the English school, we had to drive through the forests parallel to what is the main road to Angkor Wat. Apart from the occasional snake that would dart across the road, the trip there was relaxed. It was the trip home that my colleague didn't like.

We would drive home between 6:30pm and 7pm when it was already dark. When we would break from our conversation, we would hear it. Cries. Moaning. Desperation. The terrifying sounds would come from the forest and last for hundreds of metres.

My colleague would speed up the motorbike, admitting that he was terrified of ghosts. I didn't think it was ghosts; I assumed it was animals or something similar in the forest. However, one day he told me a story that made me think otherwise.

He explained that when the Khmer Rouge was in power, many bodies were buried in the forest surrounding Angkor Wat. These people had been murdered or died of disease or starvation. So, my colleague told me, they were now haunting the forest. They were souls that weren't at rest and hadn't moved on to their next lives. We had no idea what they were capable of, and my colleague certainly didn't want to find out. From that point on, I encouraged him to get me back into town as quickly as possible.

THE LAND THAT THE new Human and Hope Association community centre was built on in 2014 was empty when we leased it. Whilst the building of our community centre was going on, and right up until we opened our new premises, we hired security guards to work day and night. We needed to ensure that the building was protected and that all the construction work was going to plan.

On one of my frequent trips out to the new centre, a few weeks after the building had ceased, I arrived to find that the daytime security guard was nowhere to be seen. After looking in every room (which didn't take long, since they were open plan classrooms), my colleague called the security guard on his phone. From the back of the centre, we saw that the guard had been at a neighbour's house. He walked back to Human and Hope Association, and I accosted him as he entered through our old wire gate.

'Why weren't you here?'

'I saw a ghost, and I ran away to the neighbour's house. Don't worry, I could still watch over Human and Hope Association, and no one entered.'

'Huh? Where did you see a ghost?'

'Over there,' he pointed to the empty sewing room.

The security guard and my colleague chatted for a bit longer while I glanced around hesitantly. Once they finished, my colleague spoke to me.

'Now I understand why the night security guard quit, Sally. It is because of the ghost. He didn't want to show us he was afraid, but there is a ghost in this building. We need to get the monks to come and bless the building.'

'We are getting the monks to bless the building when we haven't had the official opening. But we can't have them come twice; it is just too much money,' I responded.

He agreed, and we put the worries of the ghost behind us. That is, until the following week...

ONE OF THE STUDENTS from the school I used to work for was a qualified electrician. We always hired him for electrical work, as we trusted his quality, and he was an inspirational young man who had turned his life around. Once Human and Hope Association's foundations were built, we needed to install electricity throughout the building, which we called my student for. He spent two weekends at Human and Hope Association, working in the scorching heat to ensure our electricity would be up and running in time for our big move.

On the second weekend of his work, I visited Human and Hope Association to say hi and check up on how things were going.

'I saw a ghost, Sally,' he told me.

'Where did you see the ghost?' I asked him.

'In the sewing room,' he responded.

When one person sees a ghost, you would probably put it down to an overly active imagination. But now this was *three* people, including one I would trust with my life, who had seen a ghost around the same room at Human and Hope Association. Something was wrong.

'What did the ghost look like?' I asked him.

'It was a shape of a person, but I didn't see the face,' he told me seriously. 'I was scared, but it is the daytime, so I am not so worried.'

I didn't know what to do. I was still hesitant to pay for the monks to come and bless the building, as we were on a tight budget and I didn't know how to justify to our Western donors that we paid twice for our building to be blessed. So, I left it and stayed clear of the sewing room when I was by myself.

MOVING DAY FINALLY ARRIVED, and it was all hands on deck to shift everything from the pagoda and set it up in time for our opening ceremony the next day. Whilst everyone was outside laying out the rocks that would eventually wash away in the rainy season, I was inside getting the office organised. My motto is *being organised is the key to success* and ensuring that everything was neat and in the right place from the beginning was of the utmost importance to me. While I was sitting at my desk sorting through documents, I saw someone on the ladder in the adjacent library, who I had assumed was my colleague, Salin. As I started to speak, I looked up and saw that there wasn't anybody on the ladder. Not wanting to jump to conclusions, I got up and walked outside, and saw that Salin was on the other side of our land, nowhere near the library. It hadn't been him on the ladder.

I went back to my desk and sat down, trying to make sense out of what I had just seen. Was it a ghost? If so, why was it there? Were we doomed to be haunted by this ghost for the duration of our 15-year land contract? While I was contemplating all things ghostly, Salin walked into the office.

'Salin, were you in here standing on the ladder before?' I asked him.

'No,' he responded.

I told him about my ghostly encounter. He stared at me, speechless.

'Oh, wow,' he eventually managed to get out.

I didn't know what to do, but I did know I was too scared to be alone in the office. For the remainder of the day, I made sure someone was always with me, so I would have a witness to the ghost and prove to myself I wasn't out of my mind. Nothing appeared again, though.

The next day we held our opening ceremony, and our community centre was blessed by Buddhist monks. We never had a ghost sighting after that.

16. Dengue, road accidents, and illnesses, oh my!

DURING ONE OF CAMBODIA'S many public holidays in 2016, my boyfriend and I decided to get out of the house for a bit. We drove along Road 6, one of the busiest roads in Cambodia, with the intention of visiting some pagodas. Along the way we pulled over to the side as a big gasoline truck was powering passed, honking its horn, and we didn't want to get taken out in the process. At that moment, while I was looking to the right, I heard a crash. I looked to my left and saw an overturned motorbike with two teenage boys sprawled on the road. We quickly parked our motorbike then made our way to where the boys were lying.

Both were injured, with one boy's bone sticking out of his left shin. Given how busy the road was, I knew the priority was to get them off the road. With my boyfriend as my translator, I organised to get both boys moved off the road without letting anyone unnecessary touch them or do more damage.

The police arrived, and an ambulance was called, with some men directing traffic around the motorbike. I stayed with the most injured boy, who turned out to

IT'S NOT ABOUT ME

be just 16 years old, trying to keep him awake, but not looking at his ghastly leg. Swarms of people made their way over to us, coming just for the 'show'; not to offer a helping hand, but just to be at the scene to look at the injuries, take photos, and have a story to tell their friends.

An ambulance eventually arrived, and they strapped the boy's leg. It was at that time I also realised that he had a hole in his upper arm.

More and more people started coming over to see the trauma, taking photos, and treating it like an outing with their friends. I finally snapped when I saw a man drive his motorbike over, get off with his iPad, and come over smiling and *laughing* to take a photo of the injured leg. When I tell someone off in Khmer, they listen. So as soon as I said to him, 'Stop photo, not good!' in front of everyone, he and a couple of others who were standing there taking a photo of this teenager in a time of need, left.

Once we knew the boys were in the ambulance, we left, trying to weave our way back to our motorbike around the 20 or so motorbikes parked on the road whose owners had decided to watch the show.

CAMBODIA IS NOT THE best place to be if you fall ill or are seriously injured. If you have travel insurance (and you *definitely* should) and are seriously injured, you will be airlifted to Thailand for medical attention.

Often when people die in Cambodia, I will ask why. The answers, apart from if they were in a motorbike accident, are never clear. 'They had a stomach ache and died,' or 'He was so tired and died.' One of our casual security guards at Human and Hope Association died in 2016, leaving his children as orphans, and I still don't understand what caused his death.

An estimated 380 people out of every 100,000 in Cambodia are infected with tuberculosis.[xv] Diarrhoeal diseases account for one fifth of the deaths of children aged five and under.[xvi] Around 32% of Cambodian children show moderate to severe stunting[xvii]. Although it can be difficult to find up-to-date statistics, I know that death is rife, judging by the number of funerals that were held in my village during my five years there.

I was often sick in Cambodia. My immune system weakened, and I was constantly battling colds, diarrhoea, food poisoning, and unexplained vomiting. Most of the time I just rode it out, but in some cases, I had to succumb to the health system in Siem Reap.

IN 2015, I WAS sitting in the office at Human and Hope Association, basking in the glory of our new internet. It could have been the excitement that came with not having to wait five minutes to load a webpage that made me overlook the mosquito buzzing near me.

That big, nasty, confident mosquito flew right over and bit me on the ankle. It was a reminder that I should be wearing mosquito repellent (it was the rainy season, after all), so I headed over to the first aid

IT'S NOT ABOUT ME

cabinet and put on some mosquito repellent we had just received as a donation.

Unfortunately, it was too little, too late.

A few days later, I couldn't get out of bed. My body ached all over, and I was unable to lift my limbs. I assumed it was from a gym workout, but looking back, I rarely worked out during my time in Cambodia (hello 30kg weight gain), so I should have known I was kidding myself.

I was working two jobs at the time; my job at Human and Hope Association, and a part-time role as an English development coordinator at another NGO to fund my job at Human and Hope Association. Although the guys at Human and Hope Association were empathetic and concerned for me, the director at my second job wasn't. I dreaded messaging him every day, telling him I was unable to make it to my two-hour a day job, as he constantly questioned my absences.

For days, I was confined to bed, experiencing symptoms such as intense lethargy, headaches, eye pains, fever, vomiting, diarrhoea, and a runny nose. It was one day, when a rash showed up, that I realised what was wrong.

That stupid mosquito had given me dengue fever.

Dengue is also known as bone crusher disease, as your bones hurt as though someone is squeezing very hard on them. It can kill people and leaves you feeling weak for some time after the worst is over.

I ended up spending two weeks in bed, sleeping 15 hours a day. I relied on my boyfriend to cook, clean, and attend to my every need. I could hardly muster up the energy to respond to an email and couldn't even concentrate on watching a movie.

Once I headed back to work, the lethargy remained and so did a headache I couldn't quite shake. I had numerous days off after that, much to the displeasure of my boss at my second job.

There was an agreement not to renew my contract for the following year.

I ONLY USED MY travel insurance once whilst I lived in Cambodia. Do I regret spending AUD$800 every year on something I barely used? Not at all. Too often I see crowdfunding campaigns for people injured on their overseas trips. Communities band together to raise tens of thousands of dollars on one individual who should have had the common sense to purchase travel insurance in the first place. If you can't afford travel insurance, you can't afford to travel.

The one time I used my travel insurance was in 2013. Preschool class had finished for the day, and it was my duty to take three of the children to their homes on my motorbike. These three children came from families who were living below the poverty line. The parents headed to work before the sun rose each day and didn't return home until long after it had set. The only way that we could recruit them into the preschool program was to offer to pick them up in the mornings (the responsibility of another teacher) and drop them home after class finished (my responsibility). Although it wasn't ideal, it was the only way to get these children attending school.

So, each day after class, I would grab three tiny sized helmets in addition to my own and race the children to my motorbike. They would fight over who would stand on the front of the motorbike and pretend to drive, while I tried to get them moving so I could get back to my work in the office.

One day, as class finished, I walked out of the office and called to the three children to follow me. As I bounced down the three steps that led from our balcony to the parking area, I slipped on a pair of shoes that were on the steps. I fell awkwardly, rolling my ankle, and landing on my back.

You know that state of shock when you know you have messed something up with your body? That is how I was feeling. My right ankle was swelling up quickly, and being no stranger to injuries, I knew that I had either badly sprained it or broken it. Having heard a crack on the way down, I assumed it was the latter.

Determined not to cry in front of these four-year-old children who were standing dazed and confused at the top of the stairs, I called out to them in Khmer.

'Go and get the teacher, go and get the teacher.'

They cocked their cute little heads to the side, continuing to stare. Then they looked back and forth at each other, trying to telepathically work out what they should be doing. They didn't get the teacher.

'Go and get the teacher, go and get the teacher,' I said again. Still, nothing.

Given we were located at a pagoda at that time, there were plenty of monks around. From a distance, one saw me laying back on the floor, writhing in pain, and knew something was up. However, as monks aren't allowed to touch females, he wasn't able to pick me up and take me into the office. The monk called out to Heng who came out of the office to see me on the floor.

'What are you doing, Sally?' he asked as if I was voluntarily laying in the dirt.

'I hurt my ankle,' I cried out in a trembling voice. 'You need to help me inside.'

Heng came down the stairs, successfully not tripping over as I just had, and awkwardly picked me up. As we made our way up the stairs and into the office, the three preschool students continued to just gawk at me, not quite sure what had just happened. Heng sat me down on my chair, and I said to him, 'This is what needs to happen. I need to put my foot up, I need you to get me a bandage from the first aid kit, and I need you to get me ice from the shop out front.'

Heng grabbed a plastic chair to put my foot on and handed me a bandage. I started to wrap my foot as he headed out the door to buy some ice.

My mistake was that I didn't specify what kind of ice I needed. As time went by, I learnt that I had to be very detailed with my needs, leaving no room for interpretation. As I sat in my office chair, tears in my eyes, my colleague returned.

With a huge block of ice.

I burst out crying. He placed the block of ice (think of it as the size of the four final *Harry Potter* books combined) on my chair.

'No, it needs to be wrapped,' I said, letting go of the fact that I needed ice cubes, not an ice *cube*.

'Oh,' he responded and went outside.

Heng returned with a disused monk's robe, which he wrapped around the block of ice and put on the chair. I had no choice, but to sacrilegiously rest my right foot on top of the ice.

As I sat there crying about the intense pain in my foot, the director at the time came back from wherever he had been.

'Sally, what happened?' he asked with concern.

In between sobs, I explained my fall. He took the three children home, who had moved past their bewilderment and were happily playing outside, whilst I debated whether I should go to the hospital.

What I needed was my mum's advice. However, as it was super expensive to phone Australia (my USD$0.45 of remaining phone credit just wasn't going to cut it), it was difficult for me to get in contact with her.

I sent her a Facebook message asking her to call me and sat in my chair weeping. I have never been one to take pain well, and my swollen ankle with fifty shades of purple hurt immensely. Eventually, my mum contacted me, and after discussing with my insurance company whether I would be covered, we decided I should go to the hospital. By this time, the director had returned.

'I need to go to the hospital,' I told him.

'Alright, let's go,' he replied.

Only it wasn't that easy. I needed his help to limp to my motorbike, which involved going down those stupid stairs again. I awkwardly hobbled down the steps and hopped on my good leg over to my motorbike. It took some time, but I eventually managed to get on the back whilst crying out in pain, then held my right leg up, so it was elevated. The director got on the front of the motorbike and took off, whilst I tried contracting my useless core muscles to keep my leg up.

The journey was a long one, as we needed to drive slowly to avoid numerous potholes on the road. We finally arrived at the international hospital 20 minutes later, and by that time, I was dangling my right foot close to the ground as I just couldn't hold it up any longer, and it hurt too much to rest it on the foot peg.

We parked out the front, and I staggered inside. The nurses stood there while we explained that I might have a broken foot. They were dressed as if they were nurses in the 1940's – white dresses, white shoes and white caps. They could have easily gone and enrolled in a World War II naval ship then and there.

IT'S NOT ABOUT ME

I was led over to a bed and climbed on while my Director went outside and moved the motorbike. The tears started again. I was in a foreign country, I possibly had a broken foot, and there was a sign on the toilet door next to me that said, 'For customers only'.

A doctor came over to examine my foot.

'Did you fall over at Angkor Wat?' he asked me.

'No. I fell on some shoes,' I whimpered.

He examined my foot not so carefully, then determined that I would need an x-ray. I was taken into a room nearby, dazed and confused, and had an x-ray taken of my foot. Not long after returning to my bed, the doctor reappeared.

'It isn't a broken foot; it is badly sprained. I want to put you in a half cast,' he told me.

'Alright,' I responded, assuming a half cast was from my foot to just above my ankle.

As often happened with my assumptions in Cambodia, I was wrong. A half cast meant the back of my calf, my ankle and bottom of my foot was covered. The rest of my foot and lower leg was wrapped with a bandage that kept the half cast attached to it.

I was issued a pair of crutches and told I was good to go. I just had to spend a few days resting it; then it would be fine to walk on. The last time I had used crutches, I sprained my wrist from using them incorrectly and then was bitten by a horse, so I wasn't looking forward to using these.

We went to the outpatient area where I paid my USD$380 bill by credit card and received medicine to help me with the pain. On the way out to my motorbike, a security guard playing with a toy helicopter rammed his toy straight into my bad leg. He just laughed and continued his way. I was not impressed with the hospital and later found out there was no need for me to use the half cast. At least I could donate my crutches to an amputee in our village once I was done with them, so someone other than the hospital benefitted from my injury.

And that, my friends, was my first and only experience with using my travel insurance. I organised first aid training at the local children's hospital for all the staff later that year, which, fortunately, they never had to use on me.

A FEW MONTHS AFTER my team had received first aid training; we came across a situation where they were able to put it into action. It was the day of 'pre-moving', that is, when we were transporting the breakable items, such as our sewing machine, by my friend's car to our new location. We had just finished dropping off another round of items and were heading back to the pagoda. I was driving (my first time in three years, and my first time in Cambodia), with my friend in the passenger's seat beside me, and Salin and Chan behind me.

As I drove slowly along the road, determined to not splash any muddy water on school children as I had done on the drive there, I saw a woman fall off her motorbike. I stopped the car and asked my colleagues, 'Did you want to help the lady?'

'*Yes!*' they answered. 'We know first aid!'

They struggled to get out of the car, as they weren't used to using seatbelts. Thirty seconds later, they were across the road, and my friend and I sat there watching them take control of the situation with ease and confidence.

Eventually, after coming back to the car, Salin said to me, 'Sally, it is so stupid. The villagers want me to rub gasoline in the woman's wound, and they won't listen to me. And now the lady won't go to the hospital even though her leg is so bad.' I told Salin I was proud of him, and although the villagers hadn't the same knowledge he had, he shouldn't be annoyed as just one year ago, he probably would have suggested the same thing as they did. He did the best he could with the injury.

EVERY SIX MONTHS, THE staff at Human and Hope Association would embark on a team building trip to a new destination in Cambodia. In 2014, we decided to head outside of Siem Reap, with Beng Mealea, Koh Ker, and Preah Vihear temples on our agenda.

These temples were so far away that I needed a passport to gain access to Preah Vihear, as it bordered with Thailand. Honestly, I don't know why I suggested this mammoth journey when I had developed car sickness during my first year in Cambodia. I should have known better.

Everything was going smoothly until I was overcome with a headache when we were at our final destination, Preah Vihear. I had hardly eaten that day, so assuming the headache was brought on by heat and a lack of food, I bought some fried egg with rice before we made our way back down the steep mountain.

Once we were in the van, I tucked into my greasy fried egg and rice. My headache started to subside, and I was feeling good. For 30 minutes or so. I suddenly became very nauseous and called out to a colleague for a plastic bag; I grabbed it just in time to throw up that delicious fried egg and rice. Again, and again, and again.

A female colleague took it upon herself to administer first aid to me. That involved karate chopping my back so that the vomit would get out and pinching my arms with brute force. For five hours, I dozed in and out of consciousness, and every time I woke up, I would vomit a bit more. And with the vomiting came more karate chops and pinching.

At one point, the driver stopped so I could get out and vomit in an open space. I jumped out of the van and crouched in the dirt with a plastic bag, while my colleagues came over and stood in a circle around me.

'Gah, you are all so Cambodian. Please don't stand and watch me vomit,' I said, shooing them away. A couple of key members of staff stayed with me while I continued to vomit.

We got back into the van and continued our journey to Siem Reap, arriving at almost 9pm. We stopped close to town, and my colleague's brother picked him up and drove him on his motorbike to Human and Hope Association, so he could collect my motorbike. He then picked me up, and along with another colleague, the three of us drove on my motorbike home.

The next time we went on a team building trip, I packed my own food and rode my motorbike behind the van. No food poisoning and no travel sickness resulted, though I did have to escape from monkeys who were trying to attach themselves to my motorbike.

ONE WEEKEND AFTER A trip to the lake, my friend Seiha and I came across an accident. We had been driving back through town when we came across a woman who had come off her bicycle. She was sprawled unconscious on the road, with several people surrounding her. I pulled the motorbike off to the side of the road, and my friend and I got off. We went over to the woman, where we saw an older woman rubbing tiger balm on her forehead, which I realised during my time in Cambodia was the solution for most things.

Fortunately, Seiha had also partaken in the same first aid training that the team at Human and Hope Association had, and he knew the best thing to do was to get this woman to the hospital. We carefully moved the woman and her bicycle off the road and laid her on the sidewalk. By this point, the woman had woken up and was mumbling incoherently. We borrowed her phone and Seiha contacted her mother, who told us that she didn't want us to take her daughter to the hospital; we had to bring her straight home. I was irritated at this, but there was nothing I could do. So, to comply with her mother's wishes, I put the woman in a tuk-tuk and sat next to her while Seiha rode my motorbike behind me.

I was determined to keep her conscious for the ride, so using my limited Khmer, I continuously asked the women maths questions. Around 15 minutes later, we arrived at her home, and an angry mother came out. She roughly grabbed her daughter (a grown woman) from the tuk-tuk and brought her into the house.

'Seiha, please explain to her mother that she needs to be checked at the hospital,' I told my friend.

Whilst I sat at my motorbike, with the tuk-tuk driver looking on, Seiha, a social worker, chatted with the woman's mother, pleading with her to take her daughter to the hospital. The mother refused, telling us that her daughter had mental health issues and was faking it, then went inside.

Exasperated, we put on our helmets to leave. Just as we did, the woman's aunty came over to us.

'Don't worry, I will take my niece to the hospital later,' she told us.

Seiha and I took her word for it and went on our way. It seemed that the mother was hiding her daughter because of her mental illness. It's estimated that about 40% of Cambodians suffer from mental health and psychological problems[xviii], yet it is a taboo topic and very common for people to hide their family members who have mental illnesses inside the home without adequate care or support.

We aren't sure what happened to the young woman afterwards, but one thing is for sure, there needs to be a nationwide strategy in Cambodia to reduce the stigma of mental illnesses.

A COUPLE OF MONTHS before I finished up at Human and Hope Association, I fell ill. I was constantly coughing and frequently threw up because of the force. I didn't know what was wrong with me. However, I couldn't stay at home as we needed to interview candidates to fill the accountant role at Human and Hope Association. Although we had previously hired an accountant, her husband was unhappy with her working far from town and spending extra time at Human and Hope Association for our staff workshops. He made his wife choose between him and us, so of course, she was forced to choose him.

I had been elated that I could finally be rid of the accounting aspect of my role, only to have it thrown back on my pile of responsibilities I was supposed to be handing over. We quickly moved into the recruitment process again and given the accounting role was such a crucial one, I had to be there for the interview.

We had scheduled to interview a young man one morning, and I was supposed to be asking the questions. However, I was barely conscious and struggling to speak, so Thai took over. I ended up leaving the interview and lying on the floor of the sewing room for two hours until it was over. Thai made the decision to hire the man, and I went home to pass out. The next day, at the expense of Human and Hope Association's staff health fund, I visited a local clinic. I was diagnosed with pneumonia, most probably because of the dirt I inhaled on my daily commute, the doctor told me.

I thought it was something I could kick quickly, however, I was wrong. We had to reschedule our accountant's induction twice, until two weeks later when I was well enough to get back to work. Hence, my departure date from Human and Hope Association was pushed back a week into July.

17. SO, you want to volunteer

THROUGHOUT THIS BOOK I have spoken about the importance of local staff running organisations. When we focus on long-term development as opposed to voluntourism, locals are more likely to have a sense of ownership or belonging, and keep the programs and organisation going.

When I first introduced the 'no volunteers' concept to the team at Human and Hope Association, they were a bit apprehensive. Just like me, they had been sold the message that NGOs couldn't properly function without ongoing support from international volunteers. The team had been accepting short-term foreign volunteers to teach the students English, not believing in their own ability to lead the classes, despite establishing Human and Hope Association by themselves. Over the next few years, I was able to prove to them that when we invested in local staff through further education, courses, and training, they were able to gain the knowledge and skills to fulfil their roles. This, combined with their cultural knowledge and familiarity with the local community, gave them the confidence to lead Human and Hope

Association without foreign volunteers, and without me.

Could Human and Hope Association have developed into a reputable community centre had it continued to accept foreign volunteers? I honestly don't believe so. I have witnessed countless other NGOs in Cambodia stagnate because the local staff are not as engaged in their organisations as Human and Hope Association's staff are. When successes happen, the staff celebrate because they know that the accomplishments were due to their devotion to the organisation and their commitment to the community. It is their hard work that achieves the outcomes, and it has been them who have been at the centre of the organisation day in and day out since 2011.

'When we were researching how international volunteers can make a positive contribution to a cause, and avoid unintended negative outcomes, the most important factor that came up time and again was learning. Most importantly, learning from local people, especially those who are affected by the problem they are trying to solve. Although international volunteers are often portrayed as the central characters in stories of change, this is actually almost never the case. The most effective volunteers recognise that they are a small cog within an ecosystem, with local leaders as the main driving force. Volunteers that are open-minded, reflective, and who learn

from and listen to local people are the only ones able to contribute to sustainable change.'
– Claire Bennett, co-author of *Learning Service: The Essential Guide to Volunteer Travel.*

I WANT TO TALK to you about long-term volunteering. This is different than voluntourism and can be effective if it is undertaken in the correct way. There are some organisations that genuinely need help because they can't find a local with the skills required to fulfil the role. Having attempted to recruit a Cambodian fundraising manager at another organisation I worked for, I can understand that need. To apply for grants requires a high level of English (or a European language), great writing skills, strategic thinking, and partner management skills. Cambodians with those skills are currently in short supply, and those who do have that skill are most likely running organisations themselves. So, yes, there can be a great need for long-term volunteers.

I know several organisations in Cambodia who have received a constant supply of long-term volunteers. Staying for anywhere between six months and two years, these volunteers help with fundraising, marketing, program management and other tasks. However, there is no consistency. With each new volunteer comes a new strategy. And the local staff are not receiving training to take over these tasks themselves. Many of those roles *could* be held by local staff if the volunteers saw their roles as capacity building with the intention of eventually having an exit strategy and being made redundant. During my time at the school I originally worked at in Cambodia, two long-term volunteers from a government sponsored program came on board, with the intention to capacity build the organisation. I didn't see that happening at the organisation I was at, because if true capacity building was happening, wouldn't that then stop the need for additional volunteers to come from this program?

When deciding to volunteer long-term, you have a responsibility to research opportunities thoroughly and ensure the community are put first. You need to think critically about long-term volunteering, and be prepared to acknowledge that in many cases, long-term volunteers may not be needed at organisations. These are the questions you should be asking yourself and the organisation when considering a long-term volunteering role:

What are your motivations to volunteer? Be honest with yourself. Are you volunteering so you can live abroad for a while, because you think the experience would look good on your resume or you want to play with adorable children? Or do you honestly believe you have a specific set of skills that an organisation genuinely needs to develop?

Whose idea was the volunteer role? There are many for-profit companies around, who don't have collaborative partnerships with the local communities, resulting in volunteer's wishes being prioritised over local client needs. The best, most meaningful volunteer placements should be designed and led by the local community to meet the needs that they have identified. If this organisation is accepting an unlimited number of volunteers, regardless of their skills, this is voluntourism as opposed to volunteering.

Can the role be filled by a local staff member? If a local person could do your job, you could be taking jobs away from them and causing harm. Do your research to find out why this role hasn't been filled by a local person, and then be honest with yourself if you are qualified to undertake it. Sometimes, while it may be frustrating for job seekers who want to work in international development, some job advertisements will ask for a significant number of years of work experience. While this is often discouraging for job seekers, it can also safeguard the organisations from taking on unskilled workers. This is something to be mindful of.

Can a local staff member gain the knowledge they need to fulfil the role in their location? In my eyes, volunteering overseas should always involve passing on skills to local staff. I have had numerous people and companies request to run training for the staff at Human and Hope Association. Why do I say no? Because they can gain that knowledge through the local universities, training providers and governing board members. NGOs are able to support the local economy, and if the staff can access that knowledge locally, there is no need for volunteers to run training.

Would I be working directly with the community? Following on from my last point, most volunteering situations should not have you working directly with the local community. For stability and for the NGO to form a trustworthy relationship with community members, the local staff should be the faces of the organisation. Your work as a long-term volunteer should focus on working directly with staff to address knowledge and skill gaps that can't be found in country.

Does the organisation tackle the root cause of the problem? When NGOs address symptoms, they are not resolving the issue. NGOs that work to resolve the root cause of a problem (such as providing education to improve employment outcomes or holding workshops on safe sex to reduce the spread of sexually transmitted diseases) are the most sustainable.

Is the organisation reputable? Do your research to ensure the organisation has a good governance structure in place, their values align with ethical and sustainable development, and what their stance is on hiring volunteers in general.

Is there a clear succession planning? I have known many volunteers who have spent time at an NGO and tried to create processes or programs that have stopped as soon as they left. If the local staff are not involved every step of the way, there is no buy-in, meaning the program most likely won't continue. And, if you truly want to make yourself redundant, like I did, there needs to be clear succession planning in place. Not just for you to pass on your skills, but for the local staff to pass on their skills to other staff, too, so that if they leave, another volunteer won't need to come in and teach them all over again.

Are you willing to learn about the culture? No matter what country you decide to volunteer in, the chances are that the culture will be substantially different to your own. When I first visited Cambodia to volunteer, I dressed inappropriately, didn't learn the basics of the language, and didn't read up on the culture. By learning about the culture of your host country, you will be much better equipped to fulfil your volunteer role, it will prepare you in terms of resilience especially if you are placed remotely, and your local colleagues will respect you for putting in this effort.

The only short-term (think one month or less) volunteering roles that are truly needed are when disasters hit, such as earthquakes or hurricanes. These roles should only be undertaken by those who are trained in disaster relief and have the skills and experience to effectively help, otherwise they will be a hinderance. You should also be informed about what organisation you will be working with, and ensuring this organisation has a structure, credibility, and is accountable. As Richard Stupart says in his volunteer guide, '*Why you shouldn't run out to volunteer for disaster relief*, your very presence in a stretched and delicate environment places one more strain on the situation, and you need to think long and hard about minimising that impact.'[xix]

Before undertaking long-term volunteering initiatives, it is important to note whether your role will then be passed onto a local team member, eliminating the need for future long-term foreign volunteers. Of course, as previously mentioned, there are situations and certain roles where it may take years to find a suitable replacement, and a succession plan would need to be in place should that local team member decide to leave the organisation.

Human and Hope Association doesn't accept long-term volunteers, as there simply isn't a need. The team are successful fundraisers and are equipped with the skills to generate some of their own funding. They are great relationship managers, and have the support of Human and Hope Australia, their funding partner. As for their projects, they are well-equipped to develop them by themselves; there is no need for a foreigner to provide training on the best way to cultivate land (as they have been living on the land their whole lives), or how to teach English effectively (all the Teachers have attended university and keep their curriculum and teaching methods fresh), or how to work with community members (the team know the community and culture best). It is offensive and condescending to assume organisations require foreign help, so the best approach is to be thoroughly analytic, consultative, open-minded and honest when pursuing long-term volunteer roles.

IT'S NOT ABOUT ME

The best roles are those where you can make yourself redundant, just like I did. Although it is heart-breaking to leave the people you have come to know and love, you will make a much bigger impact by ensuring that your skills are passed on for generations to come.

'Local people need to be empowered and valued. When local people are empowered to help their own community and their commitment and accomplishments are valued, it is an obvious evidence to prove to the other potential beneficiaries to trust and be inspired to transform their lives and not rely on foreigners. Foreigners are encouraged to help Cambodia, however, in terms of day-to-day operations, local staff should take responsibility.'
– Loeum Salin, Human and Hope Association

IF I HAVE DETERRED even one person from partaking in voluntourism by reading this book, I will be over the moon. I want to clarify however, that I am not encouraging you *not* to help. I am encouraging you to think about how you can help in effective ways, so that your time and money is used wisely, and the people you help are able to move out of poverty in sustainable and empowering ways. We are global citizens and have a responsibility to help each other; we just need to ensure we are not inadvertently causing harm in the process. If you want to help people in low-income or lower middle-income countries (which Cambodia has now progressed to), here are some great ways you can do so.

Find a reputable NGO to support with supplies – There are many reputable NGOs who have good systems in place to use the supplies you donate in their programs, which will reduce their ongoing running costs. I have come across a few people who would rather donate supplies than money, and that is perfectly fine, just make sure that the supplies you are donating are useful and the NGO has a need.

Volunteer in your home country – There are plenty of charities who financially support overseas organisations and would love for you to help them from home. Don't think that to make a difference you need to travel to another country; your skills and time can be very valuable in your home country, just ensure that you are helping the organisation where they need it, as opposed to what you feel the organisation needs. Try and find an organisation that is purely a funding partner and doesn't get involved in the day-to-day operations of the overseas organisation they are assisting.

Advocate for a cause – One of the reasons people tend to not support international organisations is because they are unaware of the extreme situations that people face, such as sex trafficking.

To help international organisations raise awareness about their causes, and thus increase financial support, you can advocate for their issues in

Australia. This might be sharing posts on social media, writing blogs, setting up petitions, or doing something on campus to get other university students caring about the issue. You do have the power to make people listen and take action.

Make donations to reputable NGOs – NGOs are always in need of money. The best NGOs are transparent and should have annual reports online, so you can see where the money is going. Your donation should not have conditions, the NGO should be able to spend it on their ongoing costs such as salaries, rent, and petrol. I know these are 'unattractive', but organisations cannot function without their staff to teach their students, their land/buildings to provide a safe environment, and petrol to conduct outreach.

Be a responsible traveler – Travel to the countries that interest you and be a responsible traveler. Shop, dine and stay at social enterprises or ethical businesses that train community members so that they can gain stable employment. It is a great way for you to be involved in the capacity building whilst also getting some benefit!

Donate blood – Donating blood is an incredible way to help Cambodians. Angkor Hospital for Children is a free hospital for children in Siem Reap that aims to provide children with access to high quality, compassionate care wherever they live and whatever their ability to pay. They are always in need of blood donors, whether it be for an open-heart surgery patient, a child suffering from chronic haemophilia or to a survivor of a motorbike accident. The best part about this is that it doesn't cost you any money to make a big impact in a Cambodian child's life.

Buy local – When donating supplies to NGOs, I urge you to buy locally so you can support the local economy. There are always products which cannot be purchased in Cambodia, but there are many more things which *can* be purchased there. When you do so, you are contributing to the small business economy, keeping people employed and saving money.

'Regardless of intentions however, the results are often the same, with evidence showing that there are profound negative effects manifesting from using vulnerable communities in developing countries as a "classroom" for privileged Western students, who have little to offer in the way of skills or expertise and are inadvertently fueling the profitable business of voluntourism and cultural exploitation... In saying all this, I do believe that there is a place for structured, community-driven, responsible volunteering programs. Ethical volunteer programs can help raise awareness of profound inequalities affecting the world, develop more globally engaged citizens who are more self-aware, committed to social justice and positive social change, while challenging perceptions and stereotypes by improving cultural intelligence.

This can help shape the social fabric of society by dismantling Western paternalistic attitudes towards the developing world and encourage and empower peer-to-peer learning across borders, languages and cultures.'
– Vivian Chordi, International Development and Higher Education Expert

THE NEXT TIME YOU see someone fundraising for their voluntourism trip overseas, don't donate. Instead, donate to a reputable organisation. Next time someone tells you that they have a longing to go and teach English in a low-income or lower middle-income country, lend them this book. Next time you see a photo on Facebook or Tinder of someone with impoverished children, don't click like. Instead, privately message that person and ask whether they had the permission of those children's parents to place the photo on Facebook, and if they have considered that participating in poverty tourism and poverty porn takes dignity away from human beings. If you ever come across an organisation that doesn't accept foreign volunteers, commend them. They understand that voluntourism is *not* the sustainable way to helping their community and developing their organisation.

18. Celebrate Your Successes

DESPITE THE MANY CHALLENGES my team and I have faced, we also had some incredible success stories. These are Cambodians who have realised that with hard work, they can achieve more than they had ever imagined. They don't let their past challenges deter them from reaching their goals; in fact, they use the lessons and experiences to make them stronger. I could write a whole book on the incredible people that have been empowered as a direct impact from the work of Human and Hope Association, but I don't have the budget for that. Instead, I am going to focus on a few stories of people who inspire me every day.

CLAY* BEGAN STUDYING WITH us at four years of age, when we first moved Human and Hope Association to Sambour Village. It was our policy only to accept children that were five years old, so they would study for a year and transition to public school together. However, Heng had come across Clay during his outreach, and seeing the extreme poverty she was living in, decided to bring her into the program.

IT'S NOT ABOUT ME

Clay was one of two girls in the class of 10. Not only was Clay younger than the other students, she was also a lot smaller as she had been born prematurely. She would cry every day when her mother brought her to school and would often refuse to go to class. When I would take photos of the preschool students, Clay refused to smile. Her mother, a housewife who would collect rattan to make baskets, persevered. Along with Clay's teacher, they helped Clay to love learning. After a few months, Clay's behaviour started to change. She would respect her teacher in class, brush her teeth at school (something she had never done in her four years on earth), and made friends. The first time I took a photo of Clay smiling was simply magical. It represented the hard work that had been put in to make sure she was happy and felt supported. From then on, I never took a photo of her frowning again.

Clay graduated from preschool a year after her other classmates and transitioned to public school.

Her grades are good, and she still attends Human and Hope Association daily for Khmer language classes, English phonics and to read in the library.

When I returned to Cambodia in May 2018, Clay was confidently playing with other children, and had left her former self in the shadows. Her growth was remarkable, and a true testament to our education programs.

SOPHY'S STORY IS ONE that breaks my heart. It is also the one that gives me the most hope. I first met Sophy in early 2015. We had hired a sustainability assistant when we moved to our new community centre – someone to cook lunches for the staff, take care of our farm, keep our community centre relatively tidy and watch over the students. Our original sustainability assistant hadn't worked out. She had trouble with alcohol and would often not turn up for work. We were determined to help her, but as you will learn from this book, due to varying life circumstances, not everyone can be helped. Or perhaps they can, but not always at the time when your help is available.

Our community manager had previously visited Sophy's house when he was conducting assessments to bring marginalised children into our scholarship program. He had originally offered the role to Sophy. However, she was recovering from appendicitis and was unable to work. Once we let our original sustainability assistant go, Thai went back to Sophy's house. She had recovered from surgery and was eager to work with us. She still works at Human and Hope Association to this day.

Sophy wasn't given a fair chance in this world from the get-go. She grew up in a war-torn country. With the Khmer Rouge taking control of Cambodia, she and her family had very little food to eat, worked all day at risk of punishment, and didn't have access to education or medical support. When her father was killed, her family struggled to survive. Yet, Sophy was considered lucky, as she wasn't one of the two million people who perished under the regime.

Once the Khmer Rouge regime ended in 1979, Sophy's family struggled to rebuild their lives. Her mother remarried a very violent man who directed his anger towards her family. One day, despite their pleas to stop, Sophy's stepfather killed her sister with a piece of wood. Her mother spiralled into depression and died several months later.

All alone, Sophy had no option, but to continue living with her stepfather. After a few months, he married a woman who forced Sophy to work from early morning until late evening. Sophy would work in the rice field and collect rattan. With no free time and anyone to care for her, Sophy never had the opportunity to attend school.

Sophy's stepfather was killed by stepping on one of the millions of landmines left over from the war. This meant that she had to work harder than ever to support herself, and she was overcome with a feeling of helplessness.

That feeling changed when she was approached by an artisan association to work with them. Sophy learnt how to paint statues and earned a good income for her work. She was finally happy, and when she met a man in her village at age 20, she decided to get married. Sophy chose him as he didn't smoke or drink alcohol, unlike many of the men in her village.

Sophy gave birth to her first child a year after getting married. Despite being allowed by her employers to take maternity leave and return to her role, her husband didn't allow her. He was jealous that she worked away from home and expected her to stay and do housework. He began to drink and became an alcoholic. With the alcohol came violence, and Sophy's life had gone full circle.

Sophy began collecting rattan to make baskets for USD$0.25 each. She also worked on a farm and completed seasonal shifts as a builder. Despite working three jobs, her salary wasn't anywhere near as much as she made when she was a statue painter.

Sophy fell into depression, and with four children to look after, she never had a free moment. Sophy was often sick, and her hospital bills pushed her family further and further into debt. This was the time when Sophy began working at Human and Hope Association. Her husband agreed this time, since our community centre was just 300 metres from her house.

As time went by, Sophy's role developed from part-time to full-time, with her taking on additional responsibilities such as teaching in art class and promoting our organisation to the community.

Sophy's four children now study in our educational programs, including English, Khmer, preschool, art class and library. They continue to study in public school, with her eldest child already in secondary school. Sophy has learnt basic Khmer through our language classes and partakes in weekly staff development workshops and external training sessions. Through our staff savings scheme, Sophy has been able to start a chicken farm and build a well for her family to access water. Their quality of living has been steadily increasing.

We work with her husband to reduce his drinking and violence by involving him in our family happiness workshops, that highlight the types of violence and their consequences and work with the perpetrators on strategies to improve their behaviour. Sophy's husband has actively been working on changing his behaviour, and it has worked. Although I can't imagine being in Sophy's situation, I have the highest respect for her. She always puts her children first, and genuinely cares about the people who are connected to Human and Hope Association. Despite not having much money, Sophy would always buy me coconuts or give me fresh vegetables from her house. She organised for Human and Hope Association to borrow land, so we could expand our farm. She treats everyone who comes to Human and Hope Association with dignity and respect, despite not being treated that way for most of her life. In 2017, Sophy built a brick house to replace her shack. She and her family finally had a safe place to live.

I am not sure what the future holds for Sophy and her family. However, I do know that her children have already been afforded a much better life than she was, and that surely must mean something.

IT'S NOT ABOUT ME

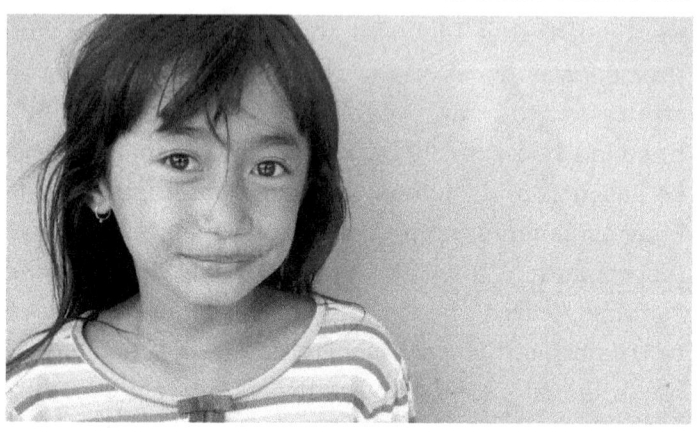

WHEN WE RECRUITED STUDENTS for a second daily preschool class in October 2013, Srey* was one of three students who joined the class. Our Education Coordinator had struggled to find students, so Srey studied in the class with just one other girl for an hour a day. Seeing that these two girls were lonely, as they only had each other to play with, our Education Coordinator decided to merge the classes and teach those 11 students for two hours a day. Despite our initial hesitation to merge classes as the original preschool class had already been studying for seven months, the two girls caught up in class.

Srey's mother would bring her to school each day by bicycle, then ride back to her rented house where she had the responsibility of watching over the mango trees for her landlord. Srey's younger sister would come along for the ride, and I would often ask that confident little girl if she wanted to study in preschool, too. She always replied yes, and I promised her mother that she could be enrolled in the preschool program when she was of the correct age.

Srey had a sullen look on her face most of the time and often disengaged in class. When I tried to talk to her, she would frequently ignore me. As time went by, Srey's behaviour improved, though her attitude did not. In October 2014, just before we moved to our new community centre, Srey graduated from our preschool program with six of her fellow students who were of age. Her mother couldn't attend the graduation and instead sent another relative. I will never forget the look on Srey's face. What should have been a glorious occasion was overshadowed by the lack of a parent.

When we moved to Sambour Commune, we lost many of our students, including Srey. She was too young at the time to ride her bicycle by herself on the dangerous, potholed main road to progress to our Khmer language classes, and her mother was unable to bring her. I never forgot my promise to Srey's mother though, and when it came time to recruit students into the 2015/16 preschool program, I asked our education manager to find Srey's mother so we could enroll her youngest daughter. The issue was though, we didn't know where Srey lived. I knew that she lived near the local market, but as our education manager didn't know Srey when she studied in preschool, it was difficult for him to identify her family. I persisted and told him that we had to fulfil my promise. A few weeks later, he successfully located

Srey's family, and her mother was thrilled for her youngest daughter to study in the preschool program.

Things hadn't been going well for Srey, however. Despite excelling academically in our preschool class, she had failed grade one and public school and was forced to repeat the class. This meant that Srey's friends would move up a grade, and she would be left behind. We encouraged Srey to attend our Khmer language class, and given her mother had to bring her sister to study in preschool at a different time, Srey was permitted to ride her bicycle to class.

Shy and under confident at first, Srey began to thrive after a few weeks. After she had studied Khmer each day, she would head to the library and read, making new friends. The next semester, Srey also added English class to her agenda. She would come to Human and Hope Association early each day and play with her new friends. She would then study in two classes, head to the library, and then head home.

When I returned to Human and Hope Association for three weeks in December 2016, Srey would confidently come up to me each day, without prompting, and greet me in the traditional Khmer fashion. I would watch as she engaged with other students in the play area, assertively answered questions in class, and had a smile plastered on her face all afternoon. I couldn't believe the transition in Srey. Despite living in poverty and facing challenges I could never comprehend, Srey had flourished into a respectful, confident, and polite girl. She continues to study at Human and Hope Association with her sister and has progressed at a public school.

SALIN WAS BORN IN Pursat Province, quite a distance from Siem Reap. At age one, his family moved to a rural area in Siem Reap; his father's hometown. Salin reflects on this time as 'awful', as his family were very poor and lived in a dilapidated cottage. His family raised cows, and Salin was responsible for looking after the cows and working in the field from a young age. During that time, they struggled to generate enough money to feed the family.

At the age of six, Salin started school. Living in a rural area, the education system was lacking, and there weren't enough teachers for the classes. Salin studied in an old building with a roof made of rusty zinc and walls made of coconut and palm leaves. When it rained, the students couldn't study as the building leaked heavily. One incident that has always stuck with Salin is being punished at school when he was naughty. His teacher hit his head with a large wooden ruler, and Salin's head swelled up. He couldn't attend school for a few days due to this injury, and his father argued with the teacher over this punishment.

IT'S NOT ABOUT ME

To give Salin the opportunity for a better education, his parents made the difficult decision to send him to live with his grandparents in Siem Reap at age eight. His grandparents were also living in poverty, so they could rarely give Salin money to support his studies. His parents and siblings then moved to Siem Reap as his father couldn't find suitable employment in their rural town. With just a small amount of money to keep them afloat, Salin's father began working as a builder, and his mother secured work as a cleaner. Living in a tiny, battered-down house, they were able to save enough money to support Salin to continue studying.

Determined to reduce the expenses his parents had to spend on his education, Salin studied hard and became one of the top students in his class. Year after year, he was rewarded with school supplies by his school in recognition of his academic achievements.

SALLY HETHERINGTON OAM

From the age of sixteen, Salin worked as a builder with his father in his free time. He used the money he earned to pay for his extra classes at school, which cost USD$35 a month, with Salin only affording USD$10. Despite being incredibly busy managing his studies, work, and home responsibilities, Salin founded Human and Hope Association with a group of his friends in grade ten. He spent one hour an evening teaching, but often his other commitments would get in his way. I remember coming across a girl in 2013 when my motorbike had broken down, who told me that Salin was her teacher, but that she had stopped studying as he was often late or didn't show up to teach.

When he was in grade eleven, seeing the potential in Salin, I sourced a university scholarship for him. I had incorrectly assumed he was in grade 12, so he was awarded a scholarship a year early! Salin was then promoted to paid employment as an English and microfinance assistant at Human and Hope Association. When he was in grade 12, my friend told me that Salin was working as a security guard at her apartment complex in the evenings. I approached Salin and enquired on whether all these commitments were overextending himself and advised that he may not be able to study properly or fulfil his work duties. He quit his evening job, but little did I know, Salin's father was sick, and his family was having financial difficulties. Salin never told me this, as he is someone who solves his problems on his own.

IT'S NOT ABOUT ME

When his grade 12 exams came around, I was certain that Salin would walk away with, at minimum, a 'B' grade, as he is highly intelligent. However, 2014 was the first year that the Cambodian government cracked down on the corrupt public education system, resulting in 75% of exam-takers, Salin included, failing the pre-requisite for getting into university. Despite being highly intelligent, Salin had decided to forgo the 'extra classes' held by his teachers, so he could work at Human and Hope Association. He missed out on crucial information that was withheld from his normal classes, and thus didn't having the knowledge to properly answer his exam questions. The government, realising what a mess this was, held six weeks of intensive classes for students who wanted to re-sit the exams. We rearranged classes at Human and Hope Association so Salin could take these lessons, and he scraped by with a pass in the next set of exams. He was able to attend university, unlike the 60% of students who ended up failing.

When Salin was working part-time, I often butted heads with him. His attitude proved to be a major problem, and I would often be left in tears of frustration. However, once he graduated from high school and began working full-time with more responsibility, his attitude, and commitment slowly changed. Salin blossomed, and his assertiveness and leadership skills developed with that.

In mid-2015, when our education and community manager suddenly resigned, I knew that Salin had the ability to step up. I discussed this with our director-in-training, Thai, who despite agreeing that Salin would be great in the position, thought that he wouldn't want to step up. I thought otherwise, and when we sat down with Salin to offer him a promotion, he hesitated ever-so-slightly before accepting. We promised we would be there with him every step of the way, and we were. From that moment until I left in 2016, I saw Salin flourish. He began developing his education team members through monthly meetings and workshops, he came up with methods to recruit and retain students, and he developed into a true leader. Nowadays, Salin is on a salary that is ten times what he originally started on. He has helped his family repair their house and assists with the education costs for his three younger siblings. He graduated from university with a Bachelor of English Literature in 2018, and the sky is the limit for him.

IT'S NOT ABOUT ME

SANGORB ALMOST DIDN'T STUDY in the sewing program at Human and Hope Association. She was approached in 2015 when our staff members were visiting the community and visiting people who lived in what can best be described as run-down houses.

When asked if she was interested in learning sewing, Sangorb told us that she had always wanted to, but never had the opportunity to do so. Sangorb was forced to stop studying at public school when she was eight years old, so she could take care of her family's buffaloes. She went on to work one job after another, but as she was illiterate, none of them paid well or brought her closer to achieving her dream of having a big house and family of her own. Sangorb eventually got married and lived in a bamboo shack with her husband. They struggled to survive from day to day, and with rain dripping through their palm leaf roof, she developed a severe skin condition.

Concerned that she couldn't attend class regularly due to her skin condition, Sangorb sadly declined the opportunity to apply for the sewing program. Determined to get Sangorb into the program, our staff referred Sangorb to an NGO that provided health services, and her skin condition was cured just in time to apply for the sewing program. She was accepted, and although it was difficult for her at first, Sangorb developed a love for sewing. She came top of her class and was hired by Human and Hope Association to make handicrafts at her home. She also developed her own sewing business, making and fixing clothes for her neighbours.

Sangorb graduated from our sewing program in October 2016 and built a gorgeous, brick home that even allowed her daughter to have her own bedroom. She set up a business at her home, which is thriving due to her high-quality craftsmanship and a low number of competitors in her area. Sangorb also works as our seamstress, making handicrafts for our sewing business, which means she can participate in our staff savings scheme and weekly capacity building workshops. Sangorb's daughter graduated from the preschool program at Human and Hope Association in 2017, and now attends public school in addition to Khmer class at Human and Hope Association. Sangorb and her husband fight much less frequently as they don't have such a financial strain anymore, and their life is a much happier one.

19. Stepping Back

THE FIRST FEW MONTHS after moving to Sambour saw some huge changes. The first was losing our major donor, who had been funding a large proportion of our organisation since day one. We were extremely grateful for her support, but the relationship had too many conditions at a time where the staff at Human and Hope Association wanted to make the move to greater autonomy, as they were ready to take full responsibility for our day-to-day operations.

I'd had a sense this had been coming and had begun to create sources of income to withstand the loss of this major income. Our sewing business was expanding, we had started to earn money from our farm, and we were constantly finding ways to reduce costs or generate money here and there. This was an important step for the independence of Human and Hope Association. We were much more financially stable without relying on such a big donor.

The situation with the donor that spanned over three years taught me a lot. I am better for it, as I never risk my integrity or the mission of Human and Hope Association for funds anymore, and recognise instances where unfortunately, certainly amazing opportunities just may not align with where we are in that point in time. I am so proud to have found individuals over the world who are joining us for this journey and will donate funds with no strings attached. If you are one of those people reading this, thank you.

MOVING TO A RURAL community, we finally had the opportunity to start a program we had sourced funding for from a while back. Our family farm program was a way to help families who had land they didn't utilise. It also aimed to start shifting away from the use of chemical fertilisers and banned pesticides, towards chemical-free vegetables. By providing families with training, knowledge, and resources, they would then be able to grow vegetables to eat or generate an income. Whatever they decided to do with the vegetables, it was a way to improve their standard of living.

We decided to conduct a six-month trial with two families, so we could work out the best way to run the program and troubleshoot any issues we came across along the way. Finding those two families was an issue. Salin, who was managing the program, spent days driving out to surrounding villages. It turned out that another organisation had conducted training in the commune a couple of years prior. They had run a three-day training session, provided the villagers with the resources they needed, and then left. There was no follow-up. All of the crops failed, and the villagers lost their confidence. They didn't want to do it again.

This was a really good lesson for Salin and the team. It demonstrated that we were playing with people's lives. If we got it wrong the first time, that person wouldn't come back for a second go. Once they 'failed', they would not give it another try, and we wouldn't be able to create an opportunity for them to break the cycle of poverty.

Eventually, Salin found two willing participants – two women who lived very close to each other. Every Sunday, Salin headed to the house of one of the students and trained them in farming techniques and other topics such as money management and business skills. It was a way for us to expand our life skills classes to the community.

Teaching the students who had not been in any sort of education for quite some time was challenging. Salin persevered, and would still turn up each week, alternating between theoretical and practical work. The hardest thing was changing the students' mindsets about growing vegetables without chemicals and pesticides. The students borrowed the funds for seeds, which they paid back interest-free over the course of the program. We also offered them tools, however, they didn't have a need for it.

Three months into the trial, one of our student's daughters fell seriously ill with a swollen brain. Her mother had to stop studying to take care of her at the hospital, leaving us with just one student. Against all odds, that student still studied solo, and her farm began to thrive. She started selling the vegetables she grew and was earning a small profit each day. Fortunately, the other student's daughter was eventually released from hospital, and she was able to join the program again. We found out that both students were still using chemicals to grow some of their vegetables, as they wanted better results. The slower, healthier approach didn't sit with them. Week after week, Salin encouraged them to ban the use of pesticides, until finally they significantly reduced the amount they used. It was the best we could do.

At the end of the six months, we evaluated, reflected, and made changes to the program. In early 2016, we launched the official, four-month program with 10 participants. Within two weeks we had to suspend it, as the drought in Siem Reap had become so severe that the students didn't have enough water to drink, let alone upkeep a farm.

AFTER A YEAR OF operating without a director, it was time to promote one of the managers to become a director-in-training. They would develop their skills for six months and then take on the directorship permanently. For the past year, part of my role was to assist our managers to hone their skills. I set expectations about what would be required from the person who took on directorship. We had learnt from our experience of the past director, and we wanted to ensure whoever took his place had the ability to continue to develop Human and Hope Association. In the constitution we had re-written from scratch, we had tentatively proposed that a director could only hold his position for two years, then there was an opportunity to uniformly change the constitution's timeframes as long as it had the full support of the board and director. There were a couple of reasons behind this. Firstly, we wanted a director to know that there was an end in sight; that he or she wouldn't always need to be at Human and Hope Association, and they would be constantly capacity building the managers so that one day they might take on the role. Secondly, we had identified a cultural issue in Cambodia, which was that people often wanted to hang onto leadership for far too long. This could cause issues for Human and Hope Association. By giving a clearly defined timeframe and an 'out', we could avoid this issue.

On a Saturday, Sreylin and I met at my house and went through all the characteristics and knowledge that the director needed to have. We rated Heng, Chan and Thai according to their ability. We wanted to make the process as fair as possible, and not show any favouritism. One by one, we discussed the strengths and weaknesses about each point in excruciating, but necessary, detail. After almost four hours, a clear winner was there. Thai was going to be the new director.

The next day, Sreylin and I with the managers. We explained the process with them and spoke about their strengths and areas of improvement. When we announced Thai as the director, there didn't seem to be much surprise. We all knew that he was the most capable. Thai was accepting of feedback; he always put Human and Hope Association first, and he was a strong leader. Although he and I have often disagreed and had arguments, he has always been the one willing to stand up to me, whilst the others shied away. And because we have a common goal – empowering our villagers to break the cycle of poverty – we have always been able to overcome our differences.

Thai began his six-months as director-in-training. As I was working with him, I began handing over my responsibilities. It wasn't difficult, as Thai had already learnt so much during the previous year. Everything was going very well, until one evening, to put it lightly, shit hit the fan.

CHECKING MY EMAIL LATE one Sunday, I came across a message from Chan to Thai and myself. He told us that he was embarrassed because although we had tried to help him a lot, he still made many mistakes with his work. He stated that he didn't want to continue to waste our funds through his scholarship, daily lunches, and salary. It was time for him to leave Human and Hope Association, he said. I put my phone down and reflected. I was shocked and saddened, because I had been encouraging and supporting him for two and a half years. I had nurtured his insecurities. I had secured external training when we identified the areas where he needed improvement. I had worked one-on-one with him because I believed in him. But, if I was being honest, that belief had started to falter over the past few months. Chan was struggling in his role running the sewing program, and I didn't see a way out of it. Thai had been working closely with him to strengthen his identified weaknesses, but he just wasn't improving. I knew his resigning wasn't ideal, but I also had to respect where he was coming from, and that in a way, Chan was empowered to do his own thing, which is what I had always wanted. I had envisaged Chan would stay with HHA, and this ended up being one of the many times when something didn't necessarily correspond with my vision, which wasn't a bad thing. So, as sad as it was that Chan wanted to leave, it was for the best.

The next morning, whilst at my teaching job, I emailed Thai and said, 'This isn't good, but I have an idea.' I then drove to Human and Hope Association and as I walked into the office, I saw Thai was the only one there. He looked exhausted.

'Did you get my email?' I asked him.

He looked at me sadly. 'Yes, but something else has happened. Let's go outside.'

We headed out to the play area and asked our students to vacate our newly built cubby house that also offered a private place for staff to talk when there weren't any children around.

'What's happened?' I asked, a thousand possibilities swimming through my head.

'Heng resigned as well,' he responded, not meeting my gaze.

I stared at him in disbelief. My heart started pounding

'What? Why?' I asked him when I was able to get my words together.

'He didn't give me a reason. He said he wanted to leave, too,' Thai replied dejectedly.

We sat in silence, reflecting on what had just happened. Both our project managers had resigned at the same time. What were the real reasons? Why was this happening?

We decided to talk to them, one at a time. I went and got Chan, who by this time, had returned to the office. He sat down with us, and we began talking.

'Chan, why do you want to resign?' I asked him. 'You said that you make many mistakes, but you also said your second reason is that it is time to leave Human and Hope Association. What does that mean?'

Chan stumbled around with his words for quite some time before telling us, 'I feel guilty about what I did to our former colleague. It is time for me to go.'

Chan was referring to an incident that led to a previous colleague's dismissal.

'Chan, if you hadn't done that, Human and Hope Association wouldn't be here today. I wouldn't be here today. This community centre wouldn't be here today.'

'It is time for me to go,' Chan repeated.

We sat there; our heads bowed. 'Okay, thank you for letting us know,' I told Chan, and watched him walk away.

We called Heng over to us. This one was going to be tougher. Even though it was always one step forward and two steps back with Heng, he was thriving in his role managing the education and community programs.

I began talking. 'Heng, Thai told me that you have resigned. Why is that?'

He looked at me. 'I was going to resign in a couple of months, but as Chan resigned now, I thought it was good if you could find two new staff at the same time. I know how difficult it was to replace Met (an English teacher) when he resigned, so it is good to do together.'

'But why do you want to resign,' I persisted.

'I cannot say,' he replied.

'But is there something we can change, or something we can do, to get you to stay?' I asked.

'No,' he responded. 'I will stay until the end of June (two months away) and then I will leave,' he told us.

'What will you do?' I asked him.

'I don't know,' he responded.

And that was that. As Heng walked away, the emotions I had been holding in for the past hour flooded out. I wept openly in front of Thai for several minutes. He sat there patiently, albeit, somewhat uncomfortably, until I composed myself.

'Sally, I don't understand. When we moved to Sambour, Heng, Chan and I made a pact with each

IT'S NOT ABOUT ME

other that we were going to commit to Human and Hope Association, and we were going to do the best job to help our community,' he told me, looking as though he was on the verge of tears, but managing to hold them in.

'I have no idea, Thai. I suppose that is their minds. And we know that there is no changing it. I feel terrible. But there is nothing we can do.'

Thai and I soon began discussing the future for those roles. It was an emotional time for us, but we had to put that aside, so the programs and students wouldn't be affected by these changes. We thought that Seyla, Human and Hope Association's sewing teacher, would be suitable to step into the role managing the program. He was good at designing products and managing product orders, and he already had good relationships with the sewing staff. Our education coordinator, Salin, had matured immensely over the past two years, and we knew he would be able to grow into that role.

Thai reflected on what we had discussed. 'These are good solutions, Sally. But do you think they will take the roles?' he asked.

'They will be surprised, and they will be hesitant. But with our encouragement, and commitment to develop their skills, they will,' I told Thai confidently.

Over the next couple of hours, Thai and I spoke to Seyla and Salin individually. As we had predicted, they were at first hesitant to step into managerial roles. However, after discussing the progress they had each made so far, and the support we were committed to giving them, they accepted the roles. We were able to replace the manager's roles with internal staff. That is the great thing about what we do at Human and Hope Association; we are constantly training up our staff so that they have the confidence to step up into roles like these. Now *that* is the beauty of empowerment.

Seyla's sewing assistant, who he had been training up over the past couple of years, was promoted to be a sewing teacher. The sewing assistant position was made redundant, so we were able to utilise some funds for other roles. We then went about hiring a full-time English teacher, Bunrong, to replace Salin. We later awarded Bunrong a university scholarship, however he sadly had to leave a few years later when he married and moved to another province. We also hired a local part-time English teacher, who stayed at the organisation for just two months. After his departure, we realised that part-time education staff just weren't working; they needed to be in the action all day, every day, to remain passionate and connected to the team. The three education team members divided the extra classes amongst themselves.

In their last weeks of work, Chan and Heng's willingness to work diminished. I often saw them working on Heng's computer together when Thai was out of the office, which arose suspicions with me since they managed different programs. It was only after their departure that it all made sense. They had gone and set up their own English school at the very pagoda we had departed due to child protection issues. Using the good name that Human and Hope Association had developed for ourselves, they recruited students from the community around the pagoda. Before he left, Heng had even told students in his English class at Human and Hope Association about the new school, and some students followed him there.

I felt as though I had been stabbed in the back. Although I could look at it as though we had supported two staff members to acquire the knowledge, confidence and skills to set up their own school, the fact that they went *back* to the place where we knew our students weren't safe, and recruited those students again, made me so disappointed that our values weren't imparted on them like I had thought, and planted a seed of doubt in my head about the effectiveness of my approach to sustainable development.

After their departure, I sometimes saw Chan riding his bicycle to the pagoda, wearing the bicycle helmet Human and Hope Association had provided him with, despite being teased by the villagers. At least that safety message still stuck with him.

FOR THE PAST COUPLE of years, we had been supporting a local public school, Buddhist Foreign Language Association, through the best method we knew how, with our knowledge. Initially, I had been running workshops with the old director on ways to improve their teaching techniques, but as time went by, Heng took over management of the program, then that was handed to Salin and Thai. They came from Kralanh, knew the community, and had a rapport with the director of the school. Every three months, they would drive the 60km out to Kralanh and delivered workshops for the teaching staff on how to deliver quality classes.

The issue they were constantly faced with was that the teaching volunteers, who were not receiving salaries, would be forced to move to Thailand to work as builders and support their family. So, they never had a consistent stream of volunteers, and knowledge was constantly being lost. We were still providing the school with a stipend for allowing the classes to be held there, but we had changed the stipdend from library books to stationery for the teachers.

As time went by, keeping Buddhist Foreign Language Association as a sub-project was becoming tedious. It would take the team a day to prepare their teaching materials, and a day to travel and hold the workshops. Already incredibly busy, they came to me one day and told me it just wasn't working anymore. The pagoda where Buddhist Foreign Language Association had originally been located had built their own school there, much like the one Human and Hope Association used in our early days, so we didn't need to support the public school with a stipend, either.

We made the decision on a Monday and were going to phone and talk to the team at Buddhist Foreign Language Association the next day. However, the next

IT'S NOT ABOUT ME

day I was contacted by Venerable Borey who told me that his team were coming to Siem Reap that very same day; they had decided to take me up on a previous offer to visit Human and Hope Association. With them already on their way, I couldn't cancel. So, that morning, six volunteers from Buddhist Foreign Language Association turned up at our door. Well, this was going to be awkward.

We permitted the volunteers to sit in the classrooms and observe the teachers, while Venerable Borey and Sokrithy (remember Sokrithy, the staff member who ran away? He was back in Cambodia and volunteering at Buddhist Foreign Language Association again) sat and chatted with the team. We told them that we would no longer be supporting the organisation; but I offered to set up a website and Facebook page for them, so they could source donors themselves. That afternoon, I worked with them and showed them the back-end of managing a WordPress site, and how to update Facebook. We still offered to be on hand to help them if they needed it, but our official relationship was over.

For one year they updated their Facebook. Unfortunately, the website was never worked on. However, at the end of the day, this was a business decision chosen by them, and that was all that mattered.

IT BECAME ROUTINE TO hold a fundraiser for my birthday each year, with all the proceeds going to

Human and Hope Association. For my 30th birthday in 2016, I set a goal to raise funds so we could hire a part-time accountant. I was successful in doing so, and in March we began recruiting. I couldn't wait; I was finally going to hand over accounting to someone else! That task had been the bane of my existence, and I didn't have the time to create a new accounting system we desperately needed.

We ended up hiring a young woman who was studying accounting at university on a scholarship from another NGO. I was hesitant, however, as we were lacking in other candidates, we decided to give her a go. I spent a week with her, teaching her our systems, running through the budget lines, and making sure she was comfortable with our policies. I had even written a whole financial policy document in one day, so she would feel comfortable with what was expected of her.

It soon became apparent that this role wasn't suited to her; she was making simple mistakes too often. This wasn't to matter though, because one month after she began, the accountant asked to speak to Thai privately and resigned. Her husband was annoyed that the workshop the evening before had gone overtime, and he had told her that either she was to resign from the job, or he would leave her. Although I was relieved that we would be able to recruit someone else, I was disturbed by this ultimatum; but there was nothing I could do.

IT'S NOT ABOUT ME

The accounting aspect at Human and Hope Association was thrown in my lap again, until we were able to hire another accountant a few weeks later. It was a blessing, really, as this accountant has done a superb job at managing the finances, and his wife is supportive if he needs to stay back late for capacity building workshops.

BEFORE I WAS TO leave Human and Hope Association, there was one program I wanted to get right. I wasn't happy with how the sewing program was going. Although Seyla and I had spent a lot of effort considerably building up the sewing business, with wholesale orders coming in from tour agencies and social enterprises, the sewing program needed a kick in the butt. It had progressed considerably over the years; however, it had now stagnated. We had created a vegetable farm which the students were responsible for and provided them with two days of food stipends a week from it. We had increased the retention rate in early 2016 thanks to a stricter contract with the students, but there was more to be done.

With Thai and Seyla, we listed the problems that we were facing with the students and came up with possible solutions, which included gender-based issues, limited resources, competition in the industry, attitudes, and limited support post-graduation.

Aside from these challenges, our teachers were also underperforming. They had been at Human and Hope

Association for three years and their quality of teaching and motivation had plateaued. Although we had tried to address issues with them before, they weren't improving. I decided to have a meeting with the team and discuss what to do. One of my suggestions was to put both teachers on performance management. Although one teacher had more concerns than the other teacher, this option seemed like our only choice. It was just a few short months until I was going to leave, and I needed to leave the sewing program in a strong position.

'When you used to talk to me about my weaknesses, I didn't pay attention. But when you gave me a warning letter, that made me change my ways. So, I think we should put them on performance management,' Salin told me.

I went about guiding Seyla and Salin on how to make performance management plans for both teachers and was clear that it would involve a lot of work from them. They would need to try their best to improve the teacher's performances, so they had a fair chance at staying in their roles. For the next few weeks, Seyla and Salin juggled their daily work with working to advance the behaviours, skills and knowledge of the teachers. Then it came time for the interim review.

Salin, Seyla, and I sat down and gave the teachers scores on each of their improvement areas. It then became obvious that one had to go. The thing was, though, this teacher was very close to the team. She was in a relationship with a staff member, like a sister to another, the former teacher of a manager, and the best friend of a board member. Despite this, it was agreed that for the best interests of Human and Hope Association and our students, she had to be let go.

This situation was one of the most challenging for staff as it put a test on their personal relationships against their commitment to Human and Hope Association, and for that I couldn't be prouder of my colleagues for their professionalism. Here we were, in a country full of nepotism, and the team were putting the best interests of the organisation over someone close to them. I was also proud of myself, who instead of forcing my opinion on the team, like I had done back in 2013 with the Davy situation, had only facilitated an open and fair conversation, encouraged them to support the teachers so that they could improve, and held my tongue while they made the difficult decision themselves. My personal growth was apparent, and I realised this journey had slowly been changing me for the better all along.

It was in that moment that I knew I was ready to leave. Human and Hope Association would be just fine without me.

I WAS TERRIFIED TO go to work on Wednesday the 6 July 2016. It was my last day at Human and Hope Association. After almost four years, I was departing. Through all the ups and downs, the waterworks, the arguments, the successes, the triumphs; this was it.

I knew that the slightest things would make me cry. I didn't want to go in. I couldn't bear to say goodbye to the team, some of whom I had been with since day one. A staff member had already given everybody the orders not to say kind words to me, or thank me, or make a big deal out of my departure, at my request. Of course, that didn't happen. The first person to break the order was our sustainability assistant, Sophy, who sent her daughter into the office to give me a coconut. Cheeky. I suppose it was her way of getting around the rule, which was smart. I still got a little teary but blinked it back. Sophy then went on to give me another two coconuts (she knew me so well) later that afternoon.

Next to break the rule was Vanna, our seamstress, who presented me with a beautiful, soft scarf, which I still have today. After that, our office team, who knew I had been eyeing our newest product, a large clutch, asked me to choose a colour then they all pitched in to buy it. But the tears still didn't come out. With all my strength, I refused to cry.

I stayed quiet during our staff lunch. We had all gathered to have a celebration, but to be honest, it didn't feel that way. Yes, I was incredibly proud that thanks to my efforts and the efforts of my team, I was able to finish up at the organisation. But there was a part of me, just like there is in everyone, who still wanted to feel needed and relevant.

With my team on my last day working at Human and Hope Association

By the end of the day, I was itching to get home to avoid anyone saying something that would result in me bawling my eyes out. Unfortunately, the skies decided to open and pour down an insane amount of rain. I sat in our study area, raincoat over my backpack and helmet over my raincoat, waiting for a break in the rain so I could make a mad dash. The rain didn't die down until 5pm. But when it did, I quickly said goodbye to the team and got on my motorbike. And as I drove out of the compound on my red and white motorbike, I burst into tears. Those tears continued on my 30-minute drive home through potholes, flood water and sticky brown mud. As I walked through the battered, wooden door of my second storey house, I sank to the floor and sobbed.

It was over. I was now redundant. They didn't need me anymore. I had dedicated almost four years to the organisation. Four years of blood, sweat, dengue fever, pneumonia, constant gastro, and tears. And it was worth every single hurdle. Every single setback. Every single sleepless night.

What I wanted to tell my team that day, but couldn't, was how proud I was of them. They have never focused on the monetary benefits of working at Human and Hope Association, which until 2017, was far below other NGOs; they focused on what they could achieve. And they have achieved a lot.

Although that part of my life was now over, it was only the beginning for Team Human and Hope Association. And boy, have they made me proud.

20. A Cambodian Love Story

I HAD NO INTENTION of falling in love in Cambodia. However, as I ended up staying there for over five years, there was a possibility of it happening. When Seyla first came for a job interview at Human and Hope Association, he was a few minutes late. Being one for punctuality, this made me put a big black mark against his name. However, the team interviewed him and agreed he should have a second interview where he would make a school uniform, so we could check the quality of his work.

A few days later, Seyla rocked up again, this time a few minutes early. The sewing machines I had ordered for him to make a school uniform on however, hadn't shown up. He sat in the second storey classroom of the pagoda, patiently waiting for the practical interview to begin, while I impatiently waited for the sewing machines to be delivered. An hour after his interview was supposed to begin, the sewing machines were delivered. Seyla set one up and got to work making a pair of school uniform shorts. Three hours later, when that classroom was meant to be used for our nightly English classes, Seyla still hadn't finished making the pants. He continued working in the room, with a wall of fabric separating him from 20 curious students, and eventually presented me with a pair of immaculately made shorts. Okay, so it had taken him much longer than we had anticipated to make the shorts, but I couldn't say a bad word about his workmanship. We decided to hire him, despite some concerns amongst the staff that having a male sewing teacher would cause jealously amongst the husbands of our sewing students.

We gave Seyla a start date, then Khmer New Year came around. I went to my friend Sreylin's house for a dinner to celebrate her mother's birthday. Whilst there, unbeknown to me, I met Seyla's mother and sister. I was introduced to them as Sreylin's aunty and cousin, though she didn't tell me that they were Seyla's relatives, nor that Sreylin was actually Seyla's first cousin. I didn't find that out until a couple of months later, when Sreylin told me, 'Although Seyla seems like a wuss, he isn't. His father was very violent, so he and his brothers learnt to be calm and quiet.'

I pressed on about why she knew this, and she confided in me that Seyla was her cousin. She had never told me, as knowing how strict I was, she didn't want me to dispel Seyla's application as a sewing teacher due to a conflict of interest.

It was challenging working with Seyla at first, as his English was limited, and my Khmer was even worse. Although I was his direct manager, I often had to communicate with him through the director, so he would understand clearly. Nowadays, Seyla tells me how much he disliked me at first. 'Your smile was so beautiful, but you were so strict and really followed the rules,' he often tells me. However, as time went on, he realised that there was a method to my madness, and he says that he and Human and Hope Association were better for it.

In August 2013, I visited Australia for the first time since moving to Cambodia. Before I left, I had half-jokingly said to Seyla at the office, 'Are you going to give me flowers to welcome me back?' and sure enough, a couple of days after I returned, he turned up to work and presented me with a dozen roses. At a cost of USD$12, these roses represented 15% of his monthly salary. I was blown away. I couldn't believe that someone had actually spent so much money on me and cared about me enough to actually make the gesture.

Upon returning, I invited my colleagues over to my house for a Khmer meal. The problem was, I had no idea how to cook any type of food, let alone Khmer food. Despite living away from my parents since 2008, I hadn't taught myself how to cook. I had been living off takeaway, hence the reason for my ongoing weight gain over the five years I was in Cambodia. Knowing I needed help, two of my colleagues met me at the local markets on the afternoon of my dinner. We perused the markets and bought everything from cutlery to pots and pans to basic ingredients. This dinner was costing me a fortune!

In the late afternoon, Seyla turned up to my house, and along with Thai, started cooking up a storm in my tiny kitchen. For the next few hours, he and Thai broke all Cambodian stereotypes and made a variety of Khmer foods whilst I watched on. Determined to contribute, I made an omelette for my team, however, as I had left out the salt, nobody was too pleased with the taste. As the night wore on, I saw Seyla in a different light. He had really come out of his shell, and was proving himself to be a caring, helpful man. In private, Sreylin asked me if I were to date anybody at work, who would it be, and in a flash the first name out of my mouth was Seyla, taking me by surprise. However, when Seyla showed me his Facebook page, I noticed photos of him playing guitar with a girl sitting next to him with a loving look on her face. I assumed he had a girlfriend, and I let my moment of weakness go. I was his manager, after all.

IN EARLY 2014, AFTER the original director left the organisation, I was no longer Seyla's direct manager, though I still had a lot of involvement with him on a day-to-day basis. As time went by, his English and confidence in speaking with me improved. Just before I left for a trip to Australia to surprise my dad for his 60th birthday, I asked my team if they would miss me. Seyla responded, 'Yes, because you are my sunshine,' and moved his hands in a big circle. It was those sorts of sweet gestures that were leading up to my realisation that I was falling in love with him.

IT'S NOT ABOUT ME

Whilst in Australia, I was shocked to open an email from Thai that read: *We are sorry to hear that Teacher Seyla had an electricity shock and felt down from his new house (4 metres) last Monday. He had a big pain to his legs and his back so much and now he cannot walk. He hasn't gone to hospital yet because he cannot stand. He is being treated by a village doctor and Khmer medicine. I just called him this morning to ask him about his situation and gave him advice to go to the hospital to check up his legs and his back bone soon.*

Seyla couldn't stand? He couldn't walk? Was he paralysed? A four-metre fall wasn't something to be taken lightly. I immediately phoned my team and told them to take him to hospital in a tuk-tuk, being very careful with how they carried him. 'Pay for all the expenses,' I told them, 'and I will find the funds to cover it.' I walked around my parent's house bewildered and worried. Cambodia wasn't the place where you would want to be injured, and I felt powerless given I wasn't there.

After a USD$94 trip to the doctor, it was discovered that Seyla had broken his foot. Although his foot was broken, and he wouldn't be able to work for quite some time, at least Seyla wasn't paralysed.

When I returned to Cambodia a few days later, I was dropped off at Human and Hope Association directly from the airport, so I could pick up my motorbike that I had left there for the team. As soon as I offloaded the goods I had bought for our programs, I headed directly to Seyla's house. As I pulled up, he was laying on a mattress in his lounge room, shirtless, wearing Angry Bird shorts with a yellowing cast on his left foot. After seeing me, he immediately put on a shirt and hobbled out to greet me on his crutches. I breathed a sigh of relief as I realised he was going to be okay.

Over the next few weeks, myself, Seyla's manager, and Seyla took two trips to a private clinic to check up on his foot. It was slow to heal, and he was no longer able to keep his nightly job as a traditional dancer, earning USD$2 a day, seven days a week. After 10 weeks, Seyla returned to work, and I was incredibly happy to see him back again. If there was a positive to come out of his injury, it was that we were able to empower his sewing assistant, Phalla, to step up into his role, and she flourished.

BEFORE WE BREAKED FOR Pchum Benh in September 2014, I was facing some issues at work. Seyla, who had taken notice of my change in demeanor, approached me on Facebook Messenger one day. He told me he wanted me to be happy, so he and our other sewing teacher were going to organise a trip to Phnom Kroam, a mountain around 15km from Siem Reap, with our sewing students.

I invited my friend, Sarah, along, and that day we met up with Seyla, a couple of staff members and our sewing students, and we then drove out to Phnom Kroam. We spent the afternoon driving our motorbikes around the mountain, playing games, and eating sweets Sarah and I had made that morning. When

IT'S NOT ABOUT ME

Sreylin made jokes about Seyla liking me, he looked at me with a cheeky grin and remained silent, not acknowledging it, but certainly not denying it. Later that evening, we all met up at a karaoke bar, and Seyla drove his motorbike next to me on the way home to ensure I got home safely.

A couple of days later, Seyla and I were talking on Facebook Messenger when I asked him to tell me something I didn't know. A few minutes went by, until a sentence popped up that would change our lives forever.

'I love you.'

I squealed, knowing that deep down, I had been waiting for a sign that Seyla was into me. Although I had suspected it for months, never in my wildest dreams did I think he would admit it.

'I love you, too,' I wrote back.

We made plans to meet up the next day and visit rural Siem Reap. Having recently purchased a microwave oven, I set about making us muffins and biscuits, which were the most basic recipes I could find.

Seyla came to my house early the next day and parked outside of my gate. I went outside to meet him and, trying to avoid any awkwardness, we made small talk before deciding to take my motorbike on the journey. The seat was wider, making for a more comfortable ride on what turned out to be a 250km round journey.

With Seyla on our first date in 2014

With me driving the motorbike, and Seyla sitting behind me, we set off to Preah Ang Choub pagoda, located on top of a mountain about 60km from Siem Reap. Very aware that I had sweat dripping down my back, I spent the drive hunched forward, hoping that Seyla's feelings for me wouldn't be diminished by the smell that was radiating off me.

Over the next few hours, we climbed a mountain, visited an ancient temple, ate my melting chocolate-chip cookies, and attempted to climb Phnom Bok, but gave up due to sheer exhaustion. Our first date was a sweat-filled day, but it didn't do anything to weaken our feelings for each other.

AFTER OUR FAILED ATTEMPT to climb Phnom Bok, we decided to try again a couple of weeks later. Seyla

IT'S NOT ABOUT ME

met me at my house one Saturday afternoon, and we made the 40-minute drive out there in relative silence. Carrying a bottle of water and wearing the traditional Khmer outfit of long pants and a jumper, I braved the sweltering humidity to stumble up the 635 steps to the top of the mountain. Every hundred steps or so, Seyla and I stopped and sat on a crumbling step to catch our breaths and hydrate. We also took the opportunity to talk. He opened to me about some family issues and sought my advice on potential ways to help. Despite my urge to give advice, I was at a loss, as this issue was one that Cambodia didn't have the resources to deal with.

We eventually made it to the top of the mountain, and I was ecstatic to realise the effort had been worth it. Not only was I getting to spend time on a blossoming relationship, I also was able to witness the miracle of nature; frangipani trees growing through the tops of dilapidated temples. After exploring, we headed back to my house, where the ingredients I had purchased at Lucky Supermarket earlier that day awaited us.

Something strange had come along with my feelings for Seyla. I had an urge to cook for him. At 28 years old, I could barely muster up basic meals for myself, yet here I was, wanting to provide him with hearty, delicious meals. So, I used my limited internet connection to research recipes that I could possibly see myself making. Whilst Seyla watched TV in my living room, I made an appetizer; four ingredient dip with avocado, tomato, coriander, and lemon. I was pretty chuffed with myself for my efforts, and although he ate some, he didn't seem as impressed as I was. Next up was a Khmer main meal. Choosing the simplest recipe, I cooked him *lok lak*, which was basically beef in sauce with onion, tomato, and rice. This was a winner, given I didn't mess it up, and Seyla devoured it. Then, for the icing on the cake (without making cake), I fried bananas with honey and sugar for dessert. By this point, we were stuffed, but out of respect, Seyla still ate a few mouthfuls (a habit he has stopped nowadays). Sitting on the couch as far away from each other as we could muster, we were watching High School Musical on my television when my housemate, Peter, walked in. I could only imagine what he was thinking when he saw this awkward scene; me, in sweaty, winter clothes on a 35-degree evening, entertaining a gentleman caller who was compelled to sit on the edge of an uncomfortable, bamboo couch, whilst slowly eating sticky banana to impress his Western love-interest, all while watching a children's musical.

'I LOVE SEYLA, BUT I don't think I can be with him,' I told my friend as we were transporting Human and Hope Association valuables from our old location to our new one.

'Why not?' she asked me.

'Well, I am clearly not going to stay in Cambodia forever,' I responded, as I swerved the car to avoid splashing some school children on bicycles with a puddle of brown, murky water. 'And the odds of getting him into Australia are stacked against us. You are aware of how difficult the process is.'

'Yes, but if you really love him, you should go for it. You can work out the visa issues. If you feel so strongly about him, it will all work out,' she responded.

At that moment, we drove past the road to Seyla's house. And there he was, on his motorbike, about to turn onto the main road we were travelling on. I waved at him and he looked at me in surprise. My heart started beating faster, I suddenly started smiling, and in that moment, I knew. I knew that this was the man I would move mountains for.

DESPITE SEYLA AND I having strong feelings for each other, we hadn't even kissed yet. Here I was, an Aussie girl who found it perfectly acceptable (and normal) to kiss strangers. Yet Seyla, at age 26, had never kissed a girl before. Every afternoon, as we left Human and Hope Association, we would ride our motorbikes next to each other until he reached the turn off to his house, and I continued onto mine. And every day, I would turn to him and ask, 'Seyla, when are you going to kiss me?'

Seyla would look at me with a sheepish grin on his face every time and shrug his shoulders. Knowing I had a trip to Australia coming up, I always reminded him that I would be away for a couple of weeks, and that he should kiss me before I go.

We continued to see each other a couple of evenings a week after work. Since I knew I had already snagged him, my efforts to cook him food had decreased, and I would instead buy us Khmer food from my favourite restaurant at the time. On those evenings we would eat food, then take my couch mattress up to the rooftop of my house and sit and talk for hours. I couldn't believe how much his English had improved since we first met; a testament to his dedication to develop himself.

Before we knew it, the evening before I flew to Australia was upon us. And finally, we were going to kiss. Seyla turned up at my house, and with his heart visibly beating through his shirt and me trying to overcome my nerves, my love had his first kiss, and we cemented our relationship.

THE NEXT DAY, BEFORE heading to Australia, I caught up with my friend and recounted Seyla's and my first kiss. Given that my friend's first kiss with her Cambodian partner had been on a motorbike, my story paled in comparison. Still, she listened carefully as I described the evening in detail, then wished me on my way as I headed back to my home country to present at a conference.

From the moment I left Cambodia, I missed Seyla. We kept in touch by Facebook, however, with his unreliable internet connection, we couldn't chat too often. Upon my return, I was offered a part-time job at a local not-for-profit whose staff member had moved onto start their own business. Although I had never considered taking another job; Human and Hope Association was my life, after all, I realised that in order to continue supporting myself in my role, and to save for Seyla's and my future, I needed to. So, after discussing firstly with Seyla, then with my colleagues at Human and Hope Association, I decided to accept the role that paid me double what I earnt at Human and Hope Association for just two hours work per day.

Afterwards, a serious talk needed to happen. Seyla and I were committed to each other, but I needed to know that he would be willing to eventually move back to Australia with me. One night soon after accepting the new role, Seyla and I spoke before eating the delicious Khmer meal I had ordered all by myself.

'Seyla, I love you, but you know I will not stay in Cambodia forever. Once I have finished my mission at Human and Hope Association, I will move back to Australia. But what I want to know is, will you be willing to move with me,' I asked him, tears slowly making their way out of my eyes.

'It makes me so happy to hear you say that,' he responded. 'I want to be with you. Although my preference is to stay in Cambodia, I will go wherever you go. So yes, I will move to Australia with you.'

With that settled, we decided we would need to move in together, sooner rather than later. *Woah*, I am sure you are thinking, *That escalated quickly.* Well, yes, in a way, it did. But keep in mind that Seyla and I had already known each other for a year and a half, we really believed our relationship would work and needed to be able to see each other in a permanent and real life. Simultaneously, I knew partner visas were notoriously difficult because they have a lot of grounds to prove – one being that we had lived together for one year. Then, once we applied, it could take up to 18 months to approve the visa, which was a year past my intended end date at Human and Hope Association. So, as you can figure, we had to get moving, both figuratively and literally.

The next day, I contacted my parents and told them Seyla and I were moving in together. They were pleasantly surprised, especially as I knew they often worried about my safety in Cambodia. A few days later, Seyla sat his parents down and told them the news. Since they already knew me and liked me (phew), they accepted his decision. I had been worried about their response since it is not culturally acceptable for couples to live together before marriage in Cambodia. However, as Rik and Thorng had an arranged marriage, they were just happy that Seyla had found someone he genuinely loved. Plus, with me being a foreigner, not a Khmer woman, the rules were a bit different, and I really appreciated his family accommodating this.

Seyla and I spent the next few weeks searching for a house we could move into on our measly budget. We eventually found a ground floor, one-bedroom apartment in a house for USD$145 a month. The landlord seemed friendly enough, so we paid the deposit and organised to move in a couple of weeks later.

SINCE SEYLA AND I worked together, and I had direct input into his performance reviews, I needed to ensure that there was to be no implied conflict of interest. We weren't keen on telling people about our relationship; the community were avid gossipers, and we just wanted to get on with our work. Therefore, we only told people on a need-to-know basis. And one of those people was Seyla's direct manager. So, one day at lunch I told his manager that Seyla and I were dating, and that I could no longer give input into Seyla's performance. He promised to keep our relationship a secret, and he kept true to his promise.

One Saturday night in February, once our exhausted team had dropped off all of our students home after participating in the Giant Puppet Parade, Seyla drove us home on his motorbike. What I had forgotten about was that our team would want to ensure that Seyla got back to his house safely once dropping me off. Thai and Salin rode beside us, and for 10 minutes I kept telling them that Seyla would be safe on his drive home and that they not need worry about him. It sounded very unlike me, so it aroused suspicion in them, but they eventually got the hint and went home.

The next day, feeling guilty about sending them on their way when they were trying to help with the best intentions, I told the other managers about Seyla's and my relationship, and that we were living together, which is why we didn't need them to drive home with him. They hid their shock quite well, congratulated me, then for months afterwards we pretended the conversation never happened.

Living together was going well, for the most part. My parents had treated us to a gym membership, so we went several (okay, perhaps two) mornings a week. We cooked separate dinners as we had differing tastes, but we always ate breakfast together. We would chill out in front of the television in our spare time, or head on road trips. The part of living together that wasn't going well was the actual apartment.

Although suitable for our budget, the apartment was full of problems. The water was inconsistent at best, with many mornings upon returning from the gym, we would find we had no water to shower. Or some evenings we would arrive home from work, dirty and sweaty, and had to go to bed in our own filth as we couldn't get water from the shower. Often, the sewage from our apartment, next door and upstairs, would regurgitate up the pipe and into our bathroom, meaning we were walking around in dirty water. And of course, the air conditioning, the main reason why we picked the apartment, didn't work 95% of the time.

We repeatedly asked the landlord to fix the issues, but he would blame us. 'The last people who lived here never had problems, it must be you. When the water doesn't work you must take the shower at different times. The bathroom is flooding because the house is bad. The air conditioner doesn't have a problem, it is just you. Why do you always complain, the people next to you never complain. You are so lucky because other landlords never help but I try to help you.'

And on it went.

Finally, Seyla, who is the type of person who never loses his cool, sat down and told the landlord that if the problems weren't fixed, we were going to have to move. The landlord just put the blame onto us again, to the point that Seyla had had enough. And so had I.

After seeking advice from friends and family, we decided for the sake of our sanity the best thing to do was to move, losing our deposit. We started looking around, and on the recommendation of my friend, ended up going through a realtor. After looking at a few houses that weren't to our liking, we found the perfect one. It was the second storey of a brand-new house, with one bedroom, two bathrooms, a kitchen, living room and balcony. It was out of our price range, however, we managed to bargain it down with the landlady from USD$305 a month to USD$255 a month. The next week, Seyla, his brothers Savdy and Sok Met, and I packed up our things into the back of a truck and told the shocked landlord we were leaving. The day after the move, whilst at the supermarket, the landlord phoned Seyla and told him that he had fixed the air conditioning. I had no idea why he did that; did he think we were suddenly going to move back in? Fortunately, our new house was comfortable, and the landlady was kind and we stayed at that house, issue free, until we left Cambodia.

IN APRIL 2015, I went on a trip to Myanmar and Singapore with my parents to celebrate my mother's 60th birthday. I moped around the whole time, missing Seyla, though not missing Cambodia as they were in the middle of a heatwave and a five-day blackout. Hence, when my parents wanted me to come and visit Australia for Christmas in 2015, it was assumed that Seyla would be coming with me.

From L to R: Srey Pov, Savdy, Rithy, Sok Met, Seyla, Sok Thet, Soky, Buntha, Rik and Thorng

We raced around to get documents to apply for a quick-turnaround passport (thanks, Mum and Dad), then once that was issued, went about the gruelling process of applying for a tourist visa into Australia. We were required to provide statutory declarations from my family that they would look after Seyla financially. We also had to prove that he was a good citizen who had commitments to return to Cambodia, to squash any concerns that he would overstay his visa. A trip to Phnom Penh and many dollars later, Seyla was issued with a tourist visa. We were headed to Australia!

Upon arriving in Australia, Seyla came down with a headache that lasted the entire three weeks. Was it culture shock? Was it the clean air with no burning of garbage? I am still not sure. Despite his constant headache, we still hit up all the tourist spots in Sydney and Newcastle, and I introduced an overwhelmed, but content, Seyla to my family and friends. After asking Seyla what his intentions were with me, Dad offered to pay for a partner application for us, which we were to get the ball rolling on when we got back to Cambodia.

The partner visa application was the most stressful process I had ever been through. We were living in a country where we didn't receive mail, didn't have phone records, and only had one Australian friend who was able to fill out a statutory declaration about our relationship. Yet, we had to fill out dozens of pages of applications and provided hundreds of pages of evidence that we truly were committed to each other.

SALLY HETHERINGTON OAM

I always tell people that the reason we were successful in our visa application is because I am an organised person. For two months, I spent every evening grasping at thin air to gather evidence from Cambodia and Australia to prove to the Australian government that our love was real. I even went so far as to print off a 200-page Facebook history, in colour. By the end of the application process, we had paid over USD$7,000 to attempt to bring Seyla into Australia on a temporary partner visa. If we had been rejected, we would have lost all that money, which was a combination of funds from both my parents and Seyla's parents, who are financially disadvantaged.

At the beginning of March 2016, weighed down with the USD$5,230 visa fee in cash, and a two-kilogram application, Seyla and I made an appointment with the visa application office and flew to Phnom Penh. On the day we submitted our application, we were a bundle of nerves. As we entered through the doors of the visa application office, we had to leave our bags with security, then wait for our number to be called. When our time finally came, we were told that a couple of the forms we had completed were out-of-date, so we frantically re-wrote them. Upon returning to the counter, the woman sorted through our documents, pulling out pages upon pages and handing them back to us, telling us we couldn't submit those particular forms. I was a wreck by the end of the process, terrified that Seyla's visa would be denied, as the visa application office was outsourced, and I wasn't confident in their process.

For months, we waited to be contacted by an immigration officer to tell us that Seyla would need to travel to Phnom Penh for a health check. Every day, we would check his email, and every day, breathe a sigh of disappointment. Finally, in June, we received news. The Department of Immigration and Border Protection wanted us to provide Seyla's police check, and evidence of his studies at high school. This was very concerning, as we had already provided his police check in the original application. Where had it gone? Were other documents then missing? My fears about the visa office had come true, and I was very anxious about it.

We emailed the Khmer staff member who had made contact, expressing concern about other missing documents. She brushed us off, telling us that it was probable that we had misplaced the documents ourselves. Given Seyla, my friend, myself, and an immigration lawyer had gone through the application with a fine-tooth comb, we were certain that wasn't the case. We contacted her again and asked for the number of statutory declarations they had received from us, as some may have gone missing, which would reduce the chances of Seyla's application being approved. When she finally got back to us, we realised that the number of statutory declarations didn't match the number we had submitted. Some *had* gone missing. Horrified, I submitted the statutory declarations again via email, and hoped that the missing documents would not affect Seyla's chances of being accepted into Australia.

We headed to Phnom Penh for Seyla's health check soon after, submitted his police check again, along with a letter stating we didn't have documents to prove his high school education, and hoped for the best. It was time to play the waiting game again and continue to prepare for the face-to-face interview we were sure to be called for.

IN JULY 2016, I visited Battambang province for an induction trip with my new workplace, having finished up at Human and Hope Association two days prior. I had taken the role so I could have a source of income whilst we waited for the visa decision to come through. For the first time in many years, I didn't have access to a computer. At 9pm that evening when we arrived back in Siem Reap, Seyla picked me up and we stopped off at Burger King on the way home for a naughty, late dinner for me.

When we arrived home, I automatically logged onto my computer whilst eating some fries and saw an email in Seyla's inbox from the Department of Immigration and Border Protection. I opened it, my heartbeat picking up its pace, assuming they were going to ask us for more documents. I opened the attachment and couldn't believe my eyes. Seyla's visa had been approved!

IT'S NOT ABOUT ME

I screamed out to Seyla in disbelief, and as he ran into our bedroom, I told him the news. We didn't believe it was true, and read and re-read the grant letter numerous times before it finally sunk in. He was accepted into Australia. It was time to go home.

21. Saying Goodbye

WE LEFT CAMBODIA ON a Monday. It was the day after my 31st birthday, which we had spent with Seyla's sister, nieces and nephews, and friends from Australia. I had spent the previous few weeks selling the mounds of possessions we had accumulated over the years, tying up loose ends and mentally preparing for the move back to Australia.

I worked at Human and Hope Association for the last three weeks I was in Cambodia, as the final part of our transition to local management. I ran workshops and refresher training, took photos, and made videos with Thai, and was basically on hand to answer any pressing questions the team had. It was clear to me that they had everything under control, and really, those last few weeks were closure for both them and I.

We held a farewell party at our house a couple of nights before we left. It was only for the staff from Human and Hope Association, and our last chance to say goodbye. Some of the male team members came over early, and spent hours cooking traditional Khmer food. As usual, my contribution was several omelettes, which people 'oohhhed' and 'aaahed' about, to keep my confidence up. This time, I remembered the salt. We sat on the floor of our living room, as all our furniture was gone. We joked and laughed and kept things light-hearted. At one point, when the team 'surprised' me with my birthday cake (I had seen them trying to sneak it into the house earlier), the lights went out and Teacher Bunrong and our accountant, Sopheak, both kissed me on my cheek, a pretty big deal for Cambodians. My team gave me presents, and took turns saying what they would miss about Seyla and I. To prevent their last memory of me being me in tears, I asked them to stop. Although I was ready to move back to Australia, I wasn't ready to let go of my team just yet. Even now, writing this, I miss them so much.

As we said goodbye, everyone tried to act as though we would be seeing them soon. But I knew that when we returned next, things would be different. Some of our seamstresses would have moved on to other jobs, other staff members would be married, and the team would be so used to not having me around that it just wouldn't be the same. However, as I have always said, my time in Cambodia at Human and Hope Association wasn't about me. Although this book documents my experience working hand-in-hand with the local team to develop the organisation, I want to be clear that I am not the hero of the story, and I never was. I played a part in supporting the team to gain the knowledge and confidence so that they could move out of poverty and show others how it could be done. I watched as this talented and passionate local created lasting change that will impact a community for generations to come. And together, we showed the world that Cambodians *do* have the ability to run their own NGOs effectively, and that this is the way forward in international development.

We spent our final morning visiting Sreylin, making my time in Cambodia into a full circle. She had been there from the beginning, and she was there at the end, too. We spent a few hours with Seyla's family, making plans to sponsor his youngest sister in English school so that hopefully she would be the first child in their family to graduate from high school and pursue a university degree. Seyla's dad gave him a water blessing, and we were taken to the airport in his aunt's car.

Although I was on the verge of tears all morning, I didn't cry. It was time to leave, to move on with my life, and encourage others to move on with theirs. Although that time of my life is over, and I do miss it terribly, leaving was the right decision. It was something that needed to be done for Human and Hope Association to thrive.

During my time in Siem Reap, I have faced an incredible amount of challenges, and have almost given up numerous times. However, I didn't. Because with every challenge has come an opportunity, and I am so proud of myself for the commitment I made to developing a grassroots NGO that is now entirely run by Cambodians. I miss the shining stars I have met, those who want to see change in their community and do something about it. I miss the women that Human and Hope Association has empowered to be confident, independent ladies who are saying no to stereotypes. And I miss the opportunities I was presented with to develop myself, whilst having a positive impact on the lives of thousands of Cambodians.

Sometimes, we must live through our mistakes so that others don't make the same ones, and it is my hope that people can grow from my own experiences with voluntourism.

We all have an important role to play, and it is time change the way we support local communities for the better.

SALLY HETHERINGTON OAM

Afterword

Human and Hope Association has continued to thrive since my departure. After I left, I was able to concentrate on fundraising and we were able to raise the staff's wages significantly. This has resulted in a much better quality of living for them all, with some even pursuing master's degrees at their own cost. The team remains focused on the outcomes of their projects and have reached some major milestones.

When the pandemic hit in early 2020, Human and Hope Association reacted quickly. They slashed their already lean budgets, the staff all took pay cuts (which have since been reinstated) to retain their jobs, and they worked with local leaders to address the most pressing needs of their community members. They reached tens of thousands of community members with COVID-19 prevention knowledge and PPE, provided emergency food packs and established a new project that has seen hundreds of families establish their own farms. As all the staff and their governing board are local, they were able to react in a timely manner and continue to support their community when other NGOs dealt with the departure of foreign staff and significant loss of income from their foreign volunteer model.

The pandemic has changed the way we work and travel forever, and it shined a light on this mode of development we have been promoting for a decade. Locals are best placed to help their communities, and we foreigners should recognise and support their journey, so it becomes the new normal.

As for Seyla and I, settling back into Australian life was tough. We arrived with just four hundred dollars to our names but, thankfully, we have a supportive family who let us live with them. I dealt with reverse culture shock, whilst Seyla had to get used to a new culture entirely. I had lost contact with many of my friends while I lived in Cambodia, but those who remained supported us through this tough transition. I continue to dedicate my life to financially supporting Human and Hope Association through Human and Hope Australia, which is a separate entity. My role now is to purely fundraise and advocate for a local approach to development. I don't get involved with Human and Hope Association's operations; I made myself redundant because as an Australian will never be best placed to run a Cambodian NGO. That needs to be left to local communities.

Even when times are tough, I don't give up. I keep persevering and will do whatever I can for the cause. That is because I know what a difference each and every dollar makes to the passionate, hard-working, capable team who are running the organisation in

Cambodia. I do it because I truly believe in the work that the team is doing, and I know that many of the people we work with will move out of poverty as a direct result of our projects and their determination.

I went to Cambodia as a girl who thought she could save the world. I came back as a woman who had played a small part in supporting a community to develop themselves. Which is so much more powerful.

Wait, I'm not finished

If you felt inspired after reading this book, sign-up to become a Monthly Champion with Human and Hope Australia. If anything, this book should have shown you that you *can* have a positive impact on the lives of Cambodians without participating in voluntourism.

A donation of $10 a month can provide a child such as Clay with access to daily education from Khmer role models, clean drinking water and a safe environment. A donation of $100 a month can help a woman like Sangorb break the cycle of poverty through a sewing program that provides them with life, business and sewing skills. And if the message of empowerment really hit home for you, a donation of $400 a month can fund the salary of a local teacher like Salin at Human and Hope Association.

Don't put off tomorrow what you can do today. Head to humanandhope.org and say 'yes' to empowerment.

Acknowledgements

People have been telling me for years that I should write a book. I have always shrugged them off, as I needed to get to it in my own time. And in early 2017, now that I was back in Australia, I finally decided the time was right. I told my best friend, Melissa Abu-Gazaleh about it, and she has encouraged me from day one, which I am very grateful for. My good friend from my school days, Andrea Britz, provided the original editing so I could get it out to publishers. Jude Irwin provided valuable advice and editing to get the book to it's first edition. Jessica Nguyen and Simon Matuzelski worked with me on the final edits. Charlie Salter listened to me whine for a year about how difficult it was to write a book and stepped up when I needed to focus. And of course, my loving partner, Seyla Thoeun, who patiently dealt with me ignoring him for months so I could get this done.

I would also like to acknowledge my mother and father, Fred and Patsy Hetherington, without whom I couldn't have survived for so long in Cambodia, and who gave Seyla and I a place to live when we returned, and all my family and friends for their encouragement over the years.

This second edition enabled me to add reflections that have developed since the book was first published in 2019. Thank you to Hannah Membrey for supporting the editing process. I continue to grow and learn and want others to know that it is never too late to change your perspective or values.

The final acknowledgement goes to you, the reader, for taking a chance on this book so you could learn from my mistakes and understand that a local approach to development is the most sustainable and empowering method for communities to thrive.

References

[i] "Religious Composition by Country, 2010-2050". *Pew Research Center's Religion & Public Life Project*, 2019, http://www.pewforum.org/2015/04/02/religious-projection-table/2010/percent/Asia-Pacific/.

[ii] World Health Organisation. *Mental Health Atlas 2005*. World Health Organisation, 2005, https://www.who.int/mental_health/evidence/atlas/profiles_countries_c_d.pdf?ua=1.

[iii] Short, Philip (2004). *Pol Pot: The History of a Nightmare*. London: John Murray. ISBN 978-0719565694.

[iv] "Khmer Rouge History | Cambodia Tribunal Monitor". *Cambodiatribunal.Org*, 2019, http://www.cambodiatribunal.org/history/cambodian-history/khmer-rouge-history/.

[v] "Transparency International - Cambodia". *Transparency.Org*, 2019, https://www.transparency.org/country/KHM.

[vi] "UNICEF - Water And Sanitation - Situation". *Unicef.Org*, 2019, https://www.unicef.org/cambodia/19061_19070.html.

[vii] Amnesty International. *Breaking The Silence: Sexual Violence In Cambodia*. 2010, p. 45, https://www.amnesty.org/download/Documents/36000/asa230012010en.pdf.

[viii] Havey, James et al. *Listening To The Demand: A Study Of Men Who Buy Sex From Female Prostitutes In Phnom Penh, Cambodia*. 2014, http://gmmiles.co.uk/wp-content/uploads/2014/05/MSF-Demand-Final-Report.pdf.

[ix] Henderson, Simon. "UN Report Says 1 In 5 Cambodian Men Have Raped". *Cambodia Daily*, 2013, https://www.cambodiadaily.com/news/un-report-says-1-in-5-cambodian-men-have-raped-42122/.

[x] Frazer, Garth. "Used-Clothing Donations And Apparel Production In Africa". *The Economic Journal*, vol 118, no. 532, 2008, pp. 1764-1784. *Oxford University Press (OUP)*, doi:10.1111/j.1468-0297.2008.02190.x.

[xi] Soenthrith, Saing. "Siem Reap Nightclub Blaze Leaves Five Dead". *The Cambodia Daily*, 2014, https://www.cambodiadaily.com/news/siem-reap-nightclub-blaze-leaves-five-dead-72602/.

[xii] Kaliyaan, Thik, and Sen David. "Fire Rips Through Siem Reap". *The Phnom Penh Post*, 2011, https://www.phnompenhpost.com/national/fire-rips-through-siem-reap.

[xiii] Sok, Kosal et al. *Cambodia Demographic And Health Survey*. The DHS Program, 2014, https://dhsprogram.com/pubs/pdf/fr312/fr312.pdf.

[xiv] Yamaguchi, Mariko. "With Birth Registrations In Hand, Local Families Secure Rights For Their Children". *UNICEF Cambodia*, 2017, http://unicefcambodia.blogspot.com/2017/02/with-birth-registrations-in-hand-local.html.

[xv] Senthilingam, Meera. "Where Health Care Is Scarce And TB Rates Are High". *CNN*, 2017, https://edition.cnn.com/2017/03/24/health/tuberculosis-cambodia-tb-day-photos/index.html.

[xvi] "UNICEF - Water And Sanitation - Situation". *Unicef.Org*, 2019, https://www.unicef.org/cambodia/19061_19070.html.

[xvii] UNICEF. *Reducing Stunting In Children Under Five Years Of Age: A Comprehensive Evaluation Of Unicef'S Strategies And Programme Performance*. UNICEF, 2017, https://www.unicef.org/cambodia/Stunting_Evaluation_Cambodia_Case_Study_Final_Report_(18_May_2017).pdf.

[xviii] De Jong, Joop (Ed.). (2002). Trauma, War and Violence. New York: Kluwer Academic/Plenum Publishers.

[xix] Stupart, Richard. "Why You Shouldn'T Run Out To Volunteer For Disaster Relief". *MATADOR Network*, 2011, https://matadornetwork.com/change/why-you-shouldnt-run-out-to-volunteer-for-disaster-relief/.

xxxiv Biddle, Pippa. 2014 https://pippabiddle.com/2014/02/18/the-problem-with-little-white-girls-and-boys/